# Contemporary Catholic Social Teaching

---

Contains

*Rerum Novarum (Pope Leo XIII)*
*Quadragesimo Anno (Pope Pius XI)*
*U.S. Bishops' Pastoral Message on the 100th*
*Anniversary of Rerum Novarum*

---

National Conference of Catholic Bishops
United States Catholic Conference

In order to commemorate the centenary of Pope Leo XIII's encyclical *Rerum Novarum*, the Office for Publishing and Promotion Services is publishing an anniversary edition that will contain, in addition to *Rerum Novarum*, *Quadragesimo Anno* and the 1990 U.S. bishops' pastoral on social teaching. This document, *Contemporary Catholic Social Teaching*, is authorized for publication by the undersigned.

Monsignor Robert N. Lynch
General Secretary
NCCB/USCC

January 18, 1991

ISBN 1-55586-401-5

Copyright © 1991 by the United States Catholic Conference, Inc.; Washington, D.C. All rights reserved. No part of this work may be reproduced or transmitted in any form or by any means, electronic or mechanical, including photocopying, recording, or by any information storage and retrieval system, without permission in writing from the copyright owner.

# Contents

**1990**  A Century of Social Teaching / 1
A Common Heritage, A Continuing Challenge

Introduction / 11
*Rev. John T. Pawlikowski, OSM, Ph.D.*

**1891**  Rerum Novarum
*On the Condition of Workers*  /  15

Introduction / 45
*Rev. John T. Pawlikowski, OSM, Ph.D.*

**1931**  Quadragesimo Anno
*On Reconstructing the Social Order*  /  47

# A Century of Social Teaching

## A Common Heritage, A Continuing Challenge

NATIONAL CONFERENCE OF CATHOLIC BISHOPS

*November 13, 1990*

Our faith calls us to work for justice; to serve those in need; to pursue peace; and to defend the life, dignity, and rights of all our sisters and brothers. This is the call of Jesus, the challenge of the prophets, and the living tradition of our Church.

Across this country and around the world, the Church's social ministry is a story of growing vitality and strength, of remarkable compassion, courage, and creativity. It is the everyday reality of providing homeless and hungry people with decent shelter and needed help, of giving pregnant women and their unborn children lifegiving alternatives, of offering refugees welcome, and so much more. It is believers advocating in the public arena for human life wherever it is threatened, for the rights of workers and for economic justice, for peace and freedom around the world, and for "liberty and justice for all" here at home. It is empowering and helping poor and vulnerable people to realize their dignity in inner cities, in rural communities and in lands far away. It is the everyday commitment of countless people, parishes and programs, local networks and national structures—a tradition of caring service, effective advocacy, and creative action.

At the heart of this commitment is a set of principles, a body of thought, and a call to action known as Catholic social teaching. In 1991, we mark the 100th anniversary of the first great modern social encyclical, *Rerum Novarum,* and celebrate a century of powerful social teaching. We recall the challenges of that new industrial age and the role of our own James Cardinal Gibbons, who encouraged Pope Leo XIII to issue this groundbreaking encyclical on work and workers. But this celebration is more than an anniversary of an important document; it is a call to share our Catholic social tradition more fully and to explore its continuing challenges for us today. This is a time for renewed reflection on our shared social tradition, a time to strengthen our common and individual commitment to work for real justice and true peace.

## Social Mission and Social Teaching

The story of the Church's social mission is both old and new, both a tradition to be shared and a challenge to be fulfilled. The Church's social ministry is:

- *founded on the life and words of Jesus Christ,* who came "to bring glad tidings to the poor . . . liberty to captives . . . recovery of sight to the blind . . ." (Lk 4:18-19), and who identified himself in the powerful parable of the Last Judgement with the hungry, the homeless, the stranger, "the least of these" (cf. Mt 25:45);
- *inspired by the passion for justice of the Hebrew prophets* and the scriptural call to care for the weak and to "let justice surge like water" (Am 5:24);
- *shaped by the social teaching of our Church,* papal encyclicals, conciliar documents, and episcopal statements that, especially over the last century, have explored, expressed, and affirmed the social demands of our faith, insisting that work for justice and peace and care for the poor and vulnerable are the responsibility of every Christian; and
- *lived by the People of God,* who seek to build up the kingdom of God, to live our faith in the world and to apply the values of the Scriptures and the teaching of the Church in our own families and parishes, in our work and service and in local communities, the nation, and the world.

The social dimensions of our faith have taken on special urgency and clarity over this last century. Guided by Pope Leo XIII and his successors, by the Second Vatican Council, and by the bishops of the Church, Catholics have been challenged to understand more clearly and act more concretely on the social demands of the gospel. This tradition calls all members of the Church, rich and poor alike, to work to eliminate the occurrence and effects of poverty, to speak out against injustice, and to shape a more caring society and a more peaceful world.

Together we seek to meet this challenge. Much, however, remains to be done if social doctrine is to become a truly vital and integral part of Catholic life and if we are to meet its challenges in our own lives and social structures. For too many, Catholic social teaching is still an unknown resource. It is sometimes misunderstood as a peripheral aspect rather than as an integral and constitutive element of our faith. The challenge of the 1971 Synod to make working for justice a constitutive dimension of responding to the gospel should be emphasized in our society, where many see religion as something personal and private. This is tragic since the Catholic social vision offers words of hope, a set of principles and directions for action to a world longing for greater freedom, justice, and peace.

Catholic social teaching is a powerful and liberating message in a world of stark contradictions: a world of inspiring new freedom and lingering oppression, of peaceful change and violent conflict, of remarkable economic progress for some and tragic misery and poverty for many others. Our teaching is a call to conscience, compassion, and creative action in a world confronting the terrible tragedy of widespread abortion, the haunting reality of hunger and homelessness, and the evil of continuing prejudice and poverty. Our teaching lifts up the moral and human dimensions of major public issues, examining "the signs of the times" through the values of the Scriptures, the teaching of the Church, and the experience of the People of God.

## Basic Themes

Our Catholic social teaching is more than a set of documents. It is a living tradition of thought and action. The Church's social vision has developed and grown over time, responding to changing circumstances and emerging problems—including developments in human work, new economic questions, war and peace in a nuclear age, and poverty and development in a shrinking world. While the subjects have changed, some basic principles and themes have emerged within this tradition.

3

## A. The Life and Dignity of the Human Person

In the Catholic social vision, the human person is central, the clearest reflection of God among us. Each person possesses a basic dignity that comes from God, not from any human quality or accomplishment, not from race or gender, age or economic status. The test of every institution or policy is whether it enhances or threatens human life and human dignity. We believe people are more important than things.

## B. The Rights and Responsibilities of the Human Person

Flowing from our God-given dignity, each person has basic rights and responsibilities. These include the rights to freedom of conscience and religious liberty, to raise a family, to immigrate, to live free from unfair discrimination, and to have a share of earthly goods sufficient for oneself and one's family. People have a fundamental right to life and to those things that make life truly human: food, clothing, housing, health care, education, security, social services, and employment. Corresponding to these rights are duties and responsibilities—to one another, to our families, and to the larger society, to respect the rights of others and to work for the common good.

## C. The Call to Family, Community, and Participation

The human person is not only sacred, but social. We realize our dignity and rights in relationship with others, in community. No community is more central than the family; it needs to be supported, not undermined. It is the basic cell of society, and the state has an obligation to support the family. The family has major contributions to make in addressing questions of social justice. It is where we learn and act on our values. What happens in the family is at the basis of a truly human social life. We also have the right and responsibility to participate in and contribute to the broader communities in society. The state and other institutions of political and economic life, with both their limitations and obligations, are instruments to protect the life, dignity, and rights of the person; promote the well-being of our families and communities; and pursue the common good. Catholic social teaching does offer clear guidance on the role of government. When basic human needs are not being met by private initiative, then people must work through their government, at appropriate levels, to meet those needs. A central test of political, legal, and economic institutions is what they do *to* people, what they do *for* people, and how people *participate* in them.

## D. The Dignity of Work and the Rights of Workers

Work is more than a way to make a living; it is an expression of our dignity and a form of continuing participation in God's creation. People have the right to decent and productive work, to decent and fair wages, to private property and economic initiative. Workers have the strong support of the Church in forming and joining union and worker associations of their choosing in the exercise of their dignity and rights. These values are at the heart of *Rerum Novarum* and other encyclicals on economic justice. In Catholic teaching, the economy exists to serve people, not the other way around.

## E. The Option for the Poor and Vulnerable

Poor and vulnerable people have a special place in Catholic social teaching. A basic moral test of a society is how its most vulnerable members are faring. This is not a new insight; it is the lesson of the parable of the Last Judgment (see Mt 25). Our tradition calls us to put the needs of the poor and vulnerable first. As Christians, we are called to respond to the needs of all our sisters and brothers, but those with the greatest needs require the greatest response. We must seek creative ways to expand the emphasis of our nation's founders on individual rights and freedom by extending democratic ideals to economic life and thus ensure that the basic requirements for life with dignity are accessible to all.

## F. Solidarity

We are one human family, whatever our national, racial, ethnic, economic, and ideological differences. We are our brothers' and sisters' keepers (cf. Gn 4:9). In a linked and limited world, our responsibilities to one another cross national and other boundaries. Violent conflict and the denial of dignity and rights to people anywhere on the globe diminish each of us. This emerging theme of solidarity, so strongly articulated by Pope John Paul II, expresses the core of the Church's concern for world peace, global development, environment, and international human rights. It is the contemporary expression of the traditional Catholic image of the *Mystical Body*. "Loving our neighbor" has global dimensions in an interdependent world.

5

There are other significant values and principles that also shape and guide the Church's traditional social teaching, but these six themes are central parts of the tradition. We encourage you to read, reflect on, and discuss the documents that make up this tradition.* They are a rich resource touching a wide variety of vital, complex, and sometimes controversial concerns. This teaching offers not an alternative social system, but fundamental values that test every system, every nation, and every community. It puts the needs of the poor first. It values persons over things. It emphasizes morality over technology, asking not simply what *can* we do, but what *ought* we do. It calls us to measure our lives not by what we have, but by who we are; how we love one another; and how we contribute to the common good, to justice in our community, and to peace in our world.

## *The Continuing Challenge*

This long tradition has led our Church over the last century to support workers and unions actively in the exercise of their rights; to work against racism and bigotry of every kind; to condemn abortion, the arms race, and other threats to human life; and to pursue a more just society and a more peaceful world. These principles are the foundation of the Catholic community's many efforts to serve the poor, immigrants, and other vulnerable people. We know our individual and institutional acts of charity are requirements of the gospel. They are essential, but not sufficient. Our efforts to feed the hungry, shelter the homeless, welcome the stranger, and serve the poor and vulnerable must be accompanied by concrete efforts to address the causes of human suffering and injustice. We believe advocacy and action to

---

\* Among the major topics addressed by these documents are a wide range of economic concerns: the roles of workers and owners; the rights to private property and its limitations; employment and unemployment; economic rights and initiative; debt and development; poverty and wealth; urban and rural concerns. Central concerns include major questions touching human life: abortion, euthanasia, health care, the death penalty, and the violence of war and crime. Also emphasized are issues of discrimination and diversity: racism, ethnic prejudice, cultural pluralism, the dignity and equality of women, and the rights of immigrants and refugees.

The teaching also addresses broader questions of religious liberty, political freedom, the common good, the role of the state, subsidiary and socialization, church-state relations, and political responsibility. A major focus has been the pursuit of peace, disarmament, the use of force and nonviolence, as well as international justice. An emerging issue is the environment.

For a fuller understanding of Catholic social teaching, see the original documents; an annotated bibliography produced by the U.S. Catholic Conference; or an excellent Vatican document, Guidelines for the Study and Teaching of the Church's Social Doctrine in the Formation of Priests (Washington, D.C.: USCC Office for Publishing and Promotion Services, 1988).

carry out our principles and constructive dialogue about how best to do this both strengthen our Church and enrich our society. We are called to transform our hearts and our social structures, to renew the face of the earth.

Social justice is not something Catholics pursue simply through parish committees and diocesan programs, although these structures can help us to act on our faith. Our social vocation takes flesh in our homes and schools, businesses and unions, offices and factories, colleges and universities, and in community organizations and professional groups. As believers, we are called to bring our values into the marketplace and the political arena, into community and family life, using our everyday opportunities and responsibilities, our voices and votes to defend human life, human dignity, and human rights. We are called to be a leaven, applying Christian values and virtues in every aspect of our lives.

We are also called to weave our social teaching into every dimension of Catholic life, especially worship, education, planning, and evangelization. The Holy Father can teach; bishops can preach; but unless our social doctrine comes alive in personal conversion and common action, it will lack real credibility and effectiveness. We need to build on the experience and commitment of so many parishes where worship consistently reflects the gospel call to continuing conversion, caring service, and creative action. The call to penance and reconciliation must include both the social and the individual dimensions of sin. Our schools and catechetical efforts should regularly share our social teaching. We know that liturgy, religious education, and other apostolates that ignore the social dimensions of our faith are neither faithful to our traditions nor fully Catholic. We also know that parish life that does not reflect the gospel call to charity and justice neglects an essential dimension of pastoral ministry. We cannot celebrate a faith we do not practice. We cannot proclaim a gospel we do not live. We must work together to ensure that we continue to move together from strong words about charity and justice to effective action, from official statements to creative ministry at every level of the Church's life.

## 1991—A Celebration and a Call

The 100th anniversary of *Rerum Novarum* is a unique opportunity to take up these challenges with new urgency and energy. We hope 1991 will be a time of deepening roots, broadening participation, and increasing collaboration on our common social mission. We urge parishes, dioceses, national organizations, and educational and other institutions to use this opportunity to share our social teaching and further integrate it into ongoing efforts. We especially ask that parishes make a major effort to celebrate and share our social teaching during this year, especially from Ascension Thursday to Pentecost Sunday, May 9-19, including May 15, the actual 100th anniversary of *Rerum Novarum* (or at some other specific time if local circumstances suggest a more appropriate date).

We are very pleased that so many people are already preparing impressive efforts to celebrate this centennial. The creative response of so many demonstrates the vitality, diversity, and unity of the Catholic community in recalling and applying our social teaching.

## Conclusion

As we celebrate this century of social teaching, it is important to remember who calls us to this task and why we pursue it. Our work for social justice is first and foremost a work of faith, a profoundly religious task. It is Jesus who calls us to this mission, not any political or ideological agenda. We are called to bring the healing hand of Christ to those in need; the courageous voice of the prophet to those in power; and the gospel message of love, justice, and peace to an often suffering world.

This is not a new challenge. It is the enduring legacy of Pope Leo XIII, who a century ago defended the rights of workers. It is the lasting message of Pope John XXIII, who called for real peace based on genuine respect for human rights. It is the continuing challenge of Pope Paul VI, who declared, "if you want peace, work for justice." It is the commitment of the Second Vatican Council, which declared, "the joys and hopes, the griefs and anxieties" of people of this age, especially those who are poor or afflicted, are "the joys and hopes, the griefs and anxieties of the followers of Christ." And it is the powerful vision of our present Holy Father, Pope John Paul II, who by word and deed calls for a new global solidarity that respects and enhances the dignity of every human person.

Most of all, it is the challenge of our Lord Jesus Christ, who laid out our continuing challenge in the Sermon on the Mount. In 1991, let us explore together what it means to be "poor in spirit" in a consumer society; to comfort those who suffer in our midst; to "show mercy" in an often unforgiving world; to "hunger and thirst for justice" in a nation still challenged by hunger and homelessness, poverty and prejudice; to be "peacemakers" in an often violent and fearful world; and to be the "salt of the earth and the light of the world" in our own time and place.

We hope and pray that, in this centennial year of *Rerum Novarum*, we will become a family of faith evermore committed to the defense of the life, the dignity, and the rights of every human person and a community of genuine solidarity, working every day to build a world of greater justice and peace for all God's children.

# Introduction to
# Rerum Novarum

The path that culminated in the first social encyclical, *Rerum Novarum*, began with a prophetic address given in 1868 to an upper-class audience in Paris by the future Cardinal Mermillod. In his remarks Mermillod tried to sensitize the ruling elites to the awful situation in which most working people found themselves. He warned that the newly emerging proletariat movement might seriously undercut the established political order in Europe unless the Catholic Church could find ways of directing the workers' outrage into constructive channels. A similar message was being voiced at the same time by other Catholic leaders like Frederic Ozanam, Augustin Cochin and Maurice Maignen.

The years 1870-71 marked a decisive turning point in the growth of Catholic social consciousness. The Franco-Prussian War and the worker insurrection known as the *Commune de Paris* threatened major destabilization in Europe. Both heightened the Church's awareness of the need to respond to the deteriorating conditions that workers faced; failure to do so might lead to massive defections to socialism. Thus, conditions were right for the development of a social doctrine that identified the Church more deeply than ever before with the struggles of the working classes.

One early influential group founded in France to address this need was the Committee for the Formation of Catholic Workers' Clubs in Paris. The *Oeuvre des Cercles* quickly attracted considerable attention throughout France, and soon inspired kindred circles in other countries. Cardinal Mermillod became a leader in one such group. In 1881 Pope Leo XIII summoned him to Rome to act as a consultant on church-state issues. Part of his task was working with a new Vatican-supported circle studying economic questions. The ideas expressed in *Rerum Novarum* first saw the light of day in this group.

Mermillod and Count Franz Kuefstein of Austria went on from this Vatican study circle to help form a new organization called the Fribourg Union in 1884. Its members shared a firm commitment to address the social crisis of the period and an equally firm loyalty to Catholic teaching and papal authority. They pledged to study the nature of work, property and society itself within the context of Thomistic

11

thought. The Union was aware that intellectual reflection alone could do little to better the condition of the working classes. They, therefore, committed themselves to pursue the enactment of international legislation reflecting the spirit of their deliberations.

Mermillod emerged as the spiritual leader of this essentially lay Catholic group. Their annual meetings between 1885 and 1891 brought together a diverse collection of Catholic thinkers from every part of Europe. While they shared some basic social ideals, the participants' political philosophies were of many shades. Staunch supporters of the aristocratic tradition rubbed shoulders with those whose allegiance lay with progressive democratic theories.

Certain questions assumed importance in the Union's discussions. The first had to do with the nature of a just wage and the proper role of the state in securing it. The Fribourg Union argued unequivocally that work is far more than a commodity. It represents a personal act of the laborer. People faithful to their work acquire a moral right to a wage sufficient to sustain themselves and their families in decency. No rigid formula was offered for defining a just wage, nor did the Union favor direct state intervention to establish one. Its members preferred freely negotiated contracts, believing that a contract that took all production costs into consideration would inevitably produce a just wage.

One clear implication of this doctrine was that workers must have the freedom to organize for collective bargaining on contracts. Only if the bargaining process broke down and workers were deprived of basic subsistence did the state have a responsibility to get involved. The Fribourg Union wished to preserve the greatest possible latitude for private initiative.

The members of the Union steered a middle course regarding state intervention and the just wage. They were open to greater intervention than liberal theorists were. They distinguished themselves from the socialists, on the other hand, by insisting on the contingent and limited nature of such intervention. *Rerum Novarum* adopted this stance almost exactly.

The Union walked the middle road on the highly controversial question of private property as well. It strongly reaffirmed the right to private ownership, laying special stress on the inviolability of the principle of private property in rural areas. In so doing, the members clearly repudiated the socialist position. Nonetheless, they did not see private property as a totally unqualified right. The right of every human being to subsistence has *primordial* status in their eyes, taking precedence over property, as fundamental as the latter remains. This analysis represented a definite break with the liberal perspective, which raised property rights to the pinnacle of social morality.

Ambiguities remained in the Union's position, and they carried over into the text of *Rerum Novarum*. Do poor people have the right to seize the property of the rich out of desperation? Does the state have the right to take over private property, with or without compensation, if such property is being used in a manner not conducive to the general welfare? The encyclical does not answer these questions.

The Fribourg Union addressed capitalism itself on many occasions. For a time, capitalism came in for harsh criticism, but in the end a more moderate outlook prevailed. Eventually the Union turned to the creation of its own distinctive social model called the *regime corporatif*. This model proposed grouping people on the basis of natural interest and social function. These groups would in turn be joined together in a larger social organism.

The Union fervently hoped that this corporate social model, which shared the organic tendencies prevalent in the medieval social vision, would end the social chaos rampant in Europe at the time, chaos the Union attributed to the influence of Enlightenment rationalism, Protestantism (which the Union felt undermined authority and encouraged irresponsible individualism) and capitalism. Fribourg's solution represented social reform rather than social revolution. Its corporate social model tried to recapture values deeply embedded in the scholastic tradition as a response to the exploitation of the working classes. Here lay the basis of its eventual appeal to Leo XIII, whose natural instincts were conservative and whose principal advisors remained committed to preservation of the aristocratic tradition. The Union's model retained the medieval spirit, even while jettisoning many of its institutions in favor of more participatory ones that benefited the working classes.

The Fribourg model, which served as the basis for *Rerum Novarum*, made a critical contribution to social thought. It recognized that social viability requires that natural and permanent groupings be endowed with some form of legal status in order to ensure the rights of all people. It is also necessary that such groups be free to express their views and that they have representation in the public domain.

This perspective laid the groundwork for Catholic commitment to the principle of union organizing. Especially in the United States, where little attention was paid to the corporate social model, the most direct and lasting effect of *Rerum Novarum* was the impulse it gave to unionization. Although a few American bishops like Cardinal Gibbons and Archbishop Ireland had already given their blessing to unionization and Catholics were already active in union leadership, the encyclical opened the doors for a much more massive and intensive collaboration between American Catholicism and the labor movement.

A dimension of the Fribourg Union's model that has taken on new importance today is its firm rejection of class struggle. The clash of social classes has become a crucial point of discussion in Catholic circles with the rise of liberation theology, especially its Latin American versions. The Vatican's concern about a "sanctification" of class struggle in such theologies has its roots in the first formulations of modern Catholic social thought.

This brief overview of the work of the Fribourg Union is essential for a full understanding not only of its child *Rerum Novarum* but also of the directions Catholic social thought has taken since. The Fribourg Union laid down certain parameters for commitment to social reform that have survived more or less intact through much of this century. They include: (1) no absolute rejection of private property; (2) no support for class struggle; (3) no formal endorsement of capitalism, a system which in many ways undercuts the organic model of society inherited from medieval thought; (4) a preferential option for the rights of workers; and (5) firm support of unionization based on a fresh interpretation of the classical organic model.

# Rerum Novarum
## On the Condition of Workers
### POPE LEO XIII

*May 15, 1891*

*To Our Venerable Brethren the Patriarchs, Primates, Archbishops, Bishops and Other Ordinaries of Places Having Peace and Communion with the Apostolic See*

Venerable Brethren
Health and Apostolic Benediction

**1.** Once the passion for revolutionary change was aroused—a passion long disturbing governments—it was bound to follow sooner or later that eagerness for change would pass from the political sphere over into the related field of economics. In fact, new developments in industry, new techniques striking out on new paths, changed relations of employer and employee, abounding wealth among a very small number and destitution among the masses, increased self-reliance on the part of workers as well as a closer bond of union with one another, and, in addition to all this, a decline in morals have caused conflict to break forth.

**2.** The momentous nature of the questions involved in this conflict is evident from the fact that it keeps men's minds in anxious expectation, occupying the talents of the learned, the discussions of the wise and experienced, the assemblies of the people, the judgment of lawmakers, and the deliberations of rulers, so that now no topic more strongly holds men's interests.

**3.** Therefore, venerable brethren, with the cause of the Church and the common welfare before us, we have thought it advisable, following our custom on other occasions when we issued to you the encyclicals *On Political Power, On Human Liberty, On the Christian Constitution of States*, and others of similar nature, which seemed opportune to refute erroneous opinions, that we ought to do the same now, and for the same reasons, *On the Condition of Workers*. We have on occasion touched more than once upon this subject. In this encyclical, however, consciousness of our apostolic office admonishes us to treat the entire question thoroughly, in order that the principles may stand out in clear light, and the conflict may thereby be brought to an end as required by truth and equity.

**4.** The problem is difficult to resolve and is not free from dangers. It is hard indeed to fix the boundaries of the rights and duties within which the rich and the proletariat—those who furnish material things and those who furnish work—ought to be restricted in relation to each other. The controversy is truly dangerous, for in various places it is being twisted by turbulent and crafty men to pervert judgment as to truth and seditiously to incite the masses.

5.   In any event, we see clearly, and all are agreed that the poor must be speedily and fittingly cared for, since the great majority of them live undeservedly in miserable and wretched conditions.

6.   After the old trade guilds had been destroyed in the last century, and no protection was substituted in their place, and when public institutions and legislation had cast off traditional religious teaching, it gradually came about that the present age handed over the workers, each alone and defenseless, to the inhumanity of employers and the unbridled greed of competitors. A devouring usury, although often condemned by the Church, but practiced nevertheless under another form by avaricious and grasping men, has increased the evil; and in addition the whole process of production as well as trade in every kind of goods has been brought almost entirely under the power of a few, so that a very few rich and exceedingly rich men have laid a yoke almost of slavery on the unnumbered masses of nonowning workers.

7.   To cure this evil, the Socialists, exciting the envy of the poor toward the rich, contend that it is necessary to do away with private possession of goods and in its place to make the goods of individuals common to all, and that the men who preside over a municipality or who direct the entire state should act as administrators of these goods. They hold that, by such a transfer of private goods from private individuals to the community, they can cure the present evil through dividing wealth and benefits equally among the citizens.

8.   But their program is so unsuited for terminating the conflict that it actually injures the workers themselves. Moreover, it is highly unjust, because it violates the rights of lawful owners, perverts the functions of the state, and throws governments into utter confusion.

9.   Clearly the essential reason why those who engage in any gainful occupation undertake labor, and at the same time the end to which workers immediately look, is to procure property for themselves and to retain it by individual right as theirs and as their very own. When the worker places his energy and his labor at the disposal of another, he does so for the purpose of getting the means necessary for livelihood. He seeks in return for the work done, accordingly, a true and full right not only to demand his wage but to dispose of it as he sees fit. Therefore, if he saves something by restricting expenditures and invests his savings in a piece of land in order to keep the fruit of his thrift more safe, a holding of this kind is certainly nothing else than his wage under a different form; and on this account land which the worker thus buys is necessarily under his full control as much as the

wage which he earned by his labor. But, as is obvious, it is clearly in this that the ownership of movable and immovable goods consists. Therefore, inasmuch as the Socialists seek to transfer the goods of private persons to the community at large, they make the lot of all wage earners worse, because in abolishing the freedom to dispose of wages they take away from them by this very act the hope and the opportunity of increasing their property and of securing advantages for themselves.

10. But, what is of more vital concern, they propose a remedy openly in conflict with justice, inasmuch as nature confers on man the right to possess things privately as his own.

11. In this respect also there is the widest difference between man and other living things. For brute beasts are not self-ruling, but are ruled and governed by a two-fold innate instinct, which not only keeps their faculty of action alert and develops their powers properly but also impels and determines their individual movements. By one instinct they are induced to protect themselves and their lives; by the other, to preserve their species. In truth, they attain both ends readily by using what is before them and within immediate range; and they cannot, of course, go further because they are moved to action by the senses alone and by the separate things perceived by the senses. Man's nature is quite different. In man there is likewise the entire and full perfection of animal nature, and consequently on this ground there is given to man, certainly no less than to every kind of living thing, to enjoy the benefits of corporeal goods. Yet animal nature, however perfectly possessed, is far from embracing human nature, but rather is much lower than human nature, having been created to serve and obey it. What stands out and excels in us, what makes man man and distinguishes him generically from the brute, is the mind or reason. And owing to the fact that this animal alone has reason, it is necessary that man have goods not only to be used, which is common to all living things, but also to be possessed by stable and perpetual right; and this applies not merely to those goods which are consumed by use, but to those also which endure after being used.

12. This is even more clearly evident, if the essential nature of human beings is examined more closely. Since man by his reason understands innumerable things, linking and combining the future with the present, and since he is master of his own actions, therefore, under the eternal law, and under the power of God most wisely ruling all things, he rules himself by the foresight of his own counsel. Wherefore it is in his power to choose the things which he considers best adapted to benefit him not only in the present but also in the future. Whence it follows that dominion not only over the fruits of the earth but also over the earth itself ought to rest in man, since he sees that things necessary for the future are furnished him out of the produce of the earth. The needs of every man are subject, as it were,

17

to constant recurrences, so that, satisfied today, they make new demands tomorrow. Therefore, nature necessarily gave man something stable and perpetually lasting on which he can count for continuous support. But nothing can give continuous support of this kind save the earth with its great abundance.

**13.** There is no reason to interpose provision by the state, for man is older than the state. Wherefore he had to possess by nature his own right to protect his life and body before any polity had been formed.

**14.** The fact that God gave the whole human race the earth to use and enjoy cannot indeed in any manner serve as an objection against private possessions. For God is said to have given the earth to mankind in common, not because he intended indiscriminate ownership of it by all, but because he assigned no part to anyone in ownership, leaving the limits of private possessions to be fixed by the industry of men and the institutions of peoples. Yet, however the earth may be apportioned among private owners, it does not cease to serve the common interest of all, inasmuch as no living being is sustained except by what the fields bring forth. Those who lack resources supply labor, so that it can be truly affirmed that the entire scheme of securing a livelihood consists in the labor which a person expends either on his own land or in some working occupation, the compensation for which is drawn ultimately from no other source than from the varied products of the earth and is exchanged for them.

**15.** For this reason it also follows that private possessions are clearly in accord with nature. The earth indeed produces in great abundance the things to preserve and, especially, to perfect life, but of itself it could not produce them without human cultivation and care. Moreover, since man expends his mental energy and his bodily strength in procuring the goods of nature, by this very act he appropriates that part of physical nature to himself which he has cultivated. On it he leaves impressed, as it were, a kind of image of his person, so that it must be altogether just that he should possess that part as his very own and that no one in any way should be permitted to violate his right.

**16.** The force of these arguments is so evident that it seems amazing that certain revivers of obsolete theories dissent from them. These men grant the individual the use of the soil and the varied fruits of the farm, but absolutely deny him the right to hold as owner either the ground on which he has built or the farm he has cultivated. When they deny this right they fail to see that a man will be defrauded of the things his labor has produced. The land, surely, that has been worked by the hand and the art of the tiller greatly changes in aspect. The wilderness is made fruitful; the barren field, fertile. But those things through which the soil has been improved so inhere in the soil and are so thoroughly intermingled with it, that they are for the most part quite inseparable from it. And, after all, would justice permit anyone to own and enjoy that upon which another has toiled? As effects follow the cause producing them, so it is just that the fruit of labor belongs precisely to those who have performed the labor.

17. Rightly therefore, the human race as a whole, moved in no wise by the dissenting opinions of a few, and observing nature carefully, has found in the law of nature itself the basis of the distribution of goods, and, by the practice of all ages, has consecrated private possession as something best adapted to man's nature and to peaceful and tranquil living together. Now civil laws, which, when just, derive their power from the natural law itself, confirm and, even by the use of force, protect this right of which we speak.—And this same right has been sanctioned by the authority of the divine law, which forbids us most strictly even to desire what belongs to another. "Thou shalt not covet thy neighbor's wife, nor his house, nor his field, nor his maid-servant, nor his ox, nor his ass, nor anything that is his."[1]

18. Rights of this kind which reside in individuals are seen to have much greater validity when viewed as fitted into and connected with the obligations of human beings in family life.

19. There is no question that in choosing a state of life it is within the power and discretion of individuals to prefer the one or the other state, either to follow the counsel of Jesus Christ regarding virginity or to bind oneself in marriage. No law of man can abolish the natural and primeval right of marriage, or in any way set aside the chief purpose of matrimony established in the beginning by the authority of God: "Increase and multiply."[2] Behold, therefore, the family, or rather the society of the household, a very small society indeed, but a true one, and older than any polity! For that reason it must have certain rights and duties of its own entirely independent of the state. Thus, right of ownership, which we have shown to be bestowed on individual persons by nature, must be assigned to man in his capacity as head of a family. Nay rather, this right is all the stronger, since the human person in family life embraces much more.

20. It is a most sacred law of nature that the father of a family see that his offspring are provided with the necessities of life, and nature even prompts him to desire to provide and to furnish his children, who, in fact reflect and in a sense continue his person, with the means of decently protecting themselves against harsh fortune in the uncertainties of life. He can do this surely in no other way than by owning fruitful goods to transmit by inheritance to his children. As already noted, the family like the state is by the same token a society in the strictest sense of the term, and it is governed by its own proper authority, namely, by that of the father. Wherefore, assuming, of

---

[1]Dt 5:21.
[2]Gn 1:28.

course, that those limits be observed which are fixed by its immediate purpose, the family assuredly possesses rights, at least equal with those of civil society, in respect to choosing and employing the things necessary for its protection and its just liberty. We say "at least equal" because, inasmuch as domestic living together is prior both in thought and in fact to uniting into a polity, it follows that its rights and duties are also prior and more in conformity with nature. But if citizens, if families, after becoming participants in common life and society, were to experience injury in a commonwealth instead of help, impairment of their rights instead of protection, society would be something to be repudiated rather than to be sought for.

21. To desire, therefore, that the civil power should enter arbitrarily into the privacy of homes is a great and pernicious error. If a family perchance is in such extreme difficulty and is so completely without plans that it is entirely unable to help itself, it is right that the distress be remedied by public aid, for each individual family is a part of the community. Similarly, if anywhere there is a grave violation of mutual rights within the family walls, public authority shall restore to each his right: for this is not usurping the rights of citizens, but protecting and confirming them with just and due care. Those in charge of public affairs, however, must stop here: nature does not permit them to go beyond these limits. Paternal authority is such that it can be neither abolished nor absorbed by the state, because it has the same origin in common with that of man's own life. "Children are a part of their father," and, as it were, a kind of extension of the father's person; and, strictly speaking, not through themselves, but through the medium of the family society in which they are begotten, they enter into and participate in civil society. And for the very reason that children "are by nature part of their father . . . before they have the use of free will, they are kept under the care of their parents."[3] Inasmuch as the Socialists, therefore, disregard care by parents and in its place introduce care by the state, they act *against natural justice* and dissolve the structure of the home.

22. And apart from the injustice involved, it is also only too evident what turmoil and disorder would obtain among all classes; and what a harsh and odious enslavement of citizens would result! The door would be open to mutual envy, detraction, and dissension. If incentives to ingenuity and skill in individual persons were to be abolished, the very fountains of wealth would necessarily dry up; and the equality conjured up by the Socialist imagination would, in reality, be nothing but uniform wretchedness and meanness for one and all, without distinction.

---

[3] St. Thomas, *Summa theologica* II-II, Q. 10, Art. 12.

**23.** From all these conversations, it is perceived that the fundamental principle of Socialism which would make all possessions public property is to be utterly rejected because it injures the very ones whom it seeks to help, contravenes the natural rights of individual persons, and throws the functions of the state and public peace into confusion. Let it be regarded, therefore, as established that in seeking help for the masses this principle before all is to be considered as basic, namely, that private ownership must be preserved inviolate. With this understood, we shall explain whence the desired remedy is to be sought.

**24.** We approach the subject with confidence and surely by our right, for the question under consideration is certainly one for which no satisfactory solution will be found unless religion and the Church have been called upon to aid. Moreover, since the safeguarding of religion and of all things within the jurisdiction of the Church is primarily our stewardship, silence on our part might be regarded as failure in our duty.

**25.** Assuredly, a question as formidable as this requires the attention and effort of others as well, namely, the heads of the state, employers and the rich, and, finally, those in whose behalf efforts are being made, the workers themselves. Yet without hesitation we affirm that if the Church is disregarded, human striving will be in vain. Manifestly, it is the Church which draws from the Gospel the teachings through which the struggle can be composed entirely or, after its bitterness is removed, can certainly become more tempered. It is the Church, again, that strives not only to instruct the mind but to regulate by her precepts the life and morals of individuals, that ameliorates the condition of the workers through her numerous and beneficient institutions, and that wishes and aims to have the thought and energy of all classes of society united to this end, that the interests of the workers be protected as fully as possible. And to accomplish this purpose she holds that the laws and the authority of the state, within reasonable limits, ought to be employed.

**26.** Therefore, let it be laid down in the first place that a condition of human existence must be borne with, namely, that in civil society the lowest cannot be made equal with the highest. Socialists, of course, agitate the contrary, but all struggling against nature is vain. There are truly very great and very many natural differences among men. Neither the talents, nor the skill, nor the health, nor the capacities of all are the same, and unequal fortune follows of itself upon necessary inequality in respect to these endowments. And clearly this condition of things is adapted to benefit both individuals and the community; for to carry on its affairs community life requires varied aptitudes and diverse services, and to perform these diverse services men are impelled most by differences in individual property holdings.

**27.** So far as bodily labor is concerned, man even before the Fall was not destined to be wholly idle; but certainly what his will at that time would have freely embraced to his soul's delight, necessity afterwards forced him to accept, with a feeling of irksomeness, for the expiation of his guilt. "Cursed be the earth in thy work: in thy labor thou shalt eat of it all the days of thy life."[4] Likewise there is to be no end on earth of other hardships, for the evil consequences of sin are hard, trying, and bitter to bear, and will necessarily accompany men even to the end of life. Therefore, to suffer and endure is human, and although men may strive in all possible ways, they will never be able by any power or art wholly to banish such tribulations from human life. If any claim they can do this, if they promise the poor in their misery a life free from all sorrow and vexation and filled with repose and perpetual pleasures, they actually impose upon these people and perpetuate a fraud which will ultimately lead to evils greater than the present. The best course is to view human affairs as they are and, as we have stated, at the same time to seek appropriate relief for these troubles elsewhere.

**28.** It is a capital evil with respect to the question we are discussing to take for granted that the one class of society is of itself hostile to the other, as if nature had set rich and poor against each other to fight fiercely in implacable war. This is so abhorrent to reason and truth that the exact opposite is true; for just as in the human body the different members harmonize with one another, whence arises that disposition of parts and proportion in the human figure rightly called symmetry, so likewise nature has commanded in the case of the state that the two classes mentioned should agree harmoniously and should properly form equally balanced counterparts to each other. Each needs the other completely: neither capital can do without labor, nor labor without capital. Concord begets beauty and order in things. Conversely, from perpetual strife there must arise disorder accompanied by bestial cruelty. But for putting an end to conflict and for cutting away its very roots, there is wondrous and multiple power in Christian institutions.

**29.** And first and foremost, the entire body of religious teaching and practice, of which the Church is the interpreter and guardian, can preeminently bring together and unite the rich and the poor by recalling the two classes of society to their mutual duties, and in particular to those duties which derive from justice.

**30.** Among these duties the following concern the poor and the workers: To perform entirely and conscientiously whatever work has been voluntarily and equitably agreed upon; not in any way to injure the property or to harm the person of employers; in protecting their own interests, to refrain from violence and never to engage in rioting; not to associate with vicious men who craftily hold out exaggerated hopes

---

[4]Gn 3:17.

and make huge promises, a course usually ending in vain regrets and in the destruction of wealth.

**31.** The following duties, on the other hand, concern rich men and employers: Workers are not to be treated as slaves; justice demands that the dignity of human personality be respected in them, ennobled as it has been through what we call the Christian character. If we hearken to natural reason and to Christian philosophy, gainful occupations are not a mark of shame to man, but rather of respect, as they provide him with an honorable means of supporting life. It is shameful and inhuman, however, to use men as things for gain and to put no more value on them than what they are worth in muscle and energy. Likewise it is enjoined that the religious interests and the spiritual well-being of the workers receive proper consideration. Wherefore, it is the duty of employers to see that the worker is free for adequate periods to attend to his religious obligations; not to expose anyone to corrupting influences or the enticements of sin, and in no way to alienate him from care for his family and the practice of thrift. Likewise, more work is not to be imposed than strength can endure, nor that kind of work which is unsuited to a worker's age or sex.

**32.** Among the most important duties of employers the principal one is to give every worker what is justly due him. Assuredly, to establish a rule of pay in accord with justice, many factors must be taken into account. But, in general, the rich and employers should remember that no laws, either human or divine, permit them for their own profit to oppress the needy and the wretched or to seek gain from another's want. To defraud anyone of the wage due him is a great crime that calls down avenging wrath from Heaven. "Behold, the wages of the laborers . . . which have been kept back by you unjustly, cry out: and their cry has entered into the ears of the Lord of Hosts."[5] Finally, the rich must religiously avoid harming in any way the savings of the workers either by coercion, or by fraud, or by the arts of usury; and the more for this reason, that the workers are not sufficiently protected against injustices and violence, and their property, being so meager, ought to be regarded as all the more sacred. Could not the observance alone of the foregoing laws remove the bitterness and the causes of conflict?

**33.** But the Church, with Jesus Christ as her teacher and leader, seeks greater things than this; namely, by commanding something more perfect, she aims at joining the two social classes to each other in closest neighborliness and friendship. We cannot understand and evaluate mortal things rightly unless the mind reflects upon the other life, the life which is immortal. If this other life indeed were taken

---

[5]Jas 5:4.

away, the form and true notion of the right would immediately perish; nay, this entire world would become an enigma insoluble to man. Therefore, what we learn from nature itself as our teacher is also a Christian dogma and on it the whole system and structure of religion rests, as it were, on its main foundation; namely, that, when we have left this life, only then shall we truly begin to live. God has not created man for the fragile and transitory things of this world, but for Heaven and eternity, and he has ordained the earth as a place of exile, not as our permanent home. Whether you abound in, or whether you lack, riches, and all the other things which are called good, is of no importance in relation to eternal happiness. But how you use them, that is truly of utmost importance. Jesus Christ by his "plentiful redemption" has by no means taken away the various tribulations with which mortal life is interwoven, but has so clearly transformed them into incentives to virtue and sources of merit that no mortal can attain eternal reward unless he follows the bloodstained footsteps of Jesus Christ. "If we endure, we shall also reign with him."[6] By the labors and suffering which he voluntarily accepted, he has wondrously lightened the burden of suffering and labor, and not only by his example but also by his grace and by holding before us the hope of eternal reward. He has made endurance of sorrows easier: "for our present light affliction, which is for the moment, prepares for us an eternal weight of glory that is beyond all measure."[7]

34. Therefore, the well-to-do are admonished that wealth does not give surcease of sorrow, and that wealth is of no avail unto the happiness of eternal life but is rather a hindrance;[8] that the threats[9] pronounced by Jesus Christ, so unusual coming from him, ought to cause the rich to fear; and that on one day the strictest account for the use of wealth must be rendered to God as Judge.

35. On the use of wealth we have the excellent and extremely weighty teaching, which, although found in a rudimentary stage in pagan philosophy, the Church has handed down in a completely developed form and causes to be observed not only in theory but in everyday life. The foundation of this teaching rests on this, that the just ownership of money is distinct from the just use of money.

36. To own goods privately, as we saw above, is a right natural to man, and to exercise this right, especially in life in society, is not only lawful, but clearly necessary. "It is lawful for man to own his own things. It is even necessary for human life."[10] But if the question be asked: How ought man use his possessions? the Church replies with-

---

[6] 2 Tm 2:12.
[7] 2 Cor 4:17.
[8] Mt 19:23-24.
[9] Lk 6:24-25.
[10] St. Thomas, *Summa theologica*, II-II, Q. 66, Art. 2.

out hesitation: "As to this point, man ought not regard external goods as his own, but as common so that, in fact, a person should readily share them when he sees others in need. Wherefore the apostle says: 'Charge the rich of this world . . . to give readily, to share with others.'"[11] No one, certainly, is obliged to assist others out of what is required for his own necessary use or for that of his family, or even to give to others what he himself needs to maintain his station in life becomingly and decently: "No one is obliged to live unbecomingly."[12] But when the demands of necessity and propriety have been sufficiently met, it is a duty to give to the poor out of that which remains. "Give that which remains as alms."[13] These are duties not of justice, except in cases of extreme need, but of Christian charity, which obviously cannot be enforced by legal action. But the laws and judgments of men yield precedence to the law and judgment of Christ the Lord, who in many ways urges the practice of alms-giving: "It is more blessed to give than to receive,"[14] and who will judge a kindness done or denied to the poor as done or denied to himself. "As long as you did it for one of these, the least of my brethren you did it for me."[15] The substance of all this is the following: whoever has received from the bounty of God a greater share of goods, whether corporeal and external, or of the soul, has received them for this purpose, namely, that he employ them for his own perfection and, likewise, as a servant of Divine Providence, for the benefit of others.

> Therefore, he that hath talent, let him constantly see to it that he be not silent; he that hath an abundance of goods, let him be on the watch that he grow not slothful in the generosity of mercy; he that hath a trade whereby he supports himself, let him be especially eager to share with his neighbor the use and benefit thereof.[16]

**37.** Those who lack fortune's goods are taught by the Church that, before God as Judge, poverty is no disgrace, and that no one should be ashamed because he makes his living by toil. And Jesus Christ has confirmed this by act and by deed, who for the salvation of men, "being rich, became poor";[17] and although he was the Son of God and God himself, yet he willed to seem and to be thought the son of a carpenter; nay, he even did not disdain to spend a great part of his life at the work of a carpenter. "Is not this the carpenter, the Son of

---

[11]Ibid. Q. 65, Art. 2.
[12]St. Thomas, *Summa theologica*, Q. 32, Art. 6.
[13]Lk 11:41.
[14]Acts 20:35.
[15]Mt 25:40.
[16]St. Gregory the Great, *In Evang. Hom.* IX, 7.
[17]2 Cor 8:9.

Mary?"[18] Those who contemplate this divine example will more easily understand these truths: True dignity and excellence in men resides in moral living, that is, in virtue; virtue is the common inheritance of man, attainable equally by the humblest and the mightiest, by the rich and the poor; and the reward of eternal happiness will follow upon virtue and merit alone, regardless of the person in whom they may be found. Nay, rather the favor of God himself seems to incline more toward the unfortunate as a class; for Jesus Christ calls the poor[19] blessed, and he invites most lovingly all who are in labor or sorrow[20] to come to him for solace, embracing with special love the lowly and those harassed by injustice. At the realization of these things the proud spirit of the rich is easily brought down, and the downcast heart of the afflicted is lifted up; the former are moved toward kindness, the latter, toward reasonableness in their demands. Thus the distance between the classes which pride seeks is reduced, and it will easily be brought to pass that the two classes, with hands clasped in friendship, will be united in heart.

38. Yet, if they obey Christian teachings, not merely friendship but brotherly love also will bind them to each other. They will feel and understand that all men indeed have been created by God, their common Father; that all strive for the same object of good, which is God himself, who alone can communicate to both men and angels perfect and absolute happiness; that all equally have been redeemed by the grace of Jesus Christ and restored to the dignity of the sons of God, so that they are clearly united by the bonds of brotherhood not only with one another but also with Christ the Lord, "the firstborn among many brethren,"[21] and further, that the goods of nature and the gifts of Divine Grace belong in common and without distinction to all human kind, and that no one, unless he is unworthy, will be deprived of the inheritance of Heaven. "But if we are sons, we are also heirs: heirs indeed of God and joint heirs with Christ."[22]

39. Such is the economy of duties and rights according to Christian philosophy. Would it not seem that all conflict would soon cease wherever this economy were to prevail in civil society?

40. Finally, the Church does not consider it enough to point out the way of finding the cure, but she administers the remedy herself. For she occupies herself fully in training and forming men according to discipline and doctrine; and through the agency of bishops and clergy, she causes the health-giving streams of this doctrine to be diffused as widely as possible. Furthermore, she strives to enter into men's

---

[18]Mk 6:3.
[19]Mt 5:3.
[20]Mt 11:28.
[21]Rom 8:29.
[22]Rom 8:17.

minds and to bend their wills so that they may suffer themselves to be ruled and governed by the discipline of the divine precepts. And in this field, which is of first and greatest importance because in it the whole substance and matter of benefits consists, the Church indeed has a power that is especially unique. For the instruments which she uses to move souls were given her for this very purpose by Jesus Christ, and they have an efficacy implanted in them by God. Such instruments alone can properly penetrate the inner recesses of the heart and lead man to obedience to duty, to govern the activities of his self-seeking mind, to love God and his neighbors with a special and sovereign love, and to overcome courageously all things that impede the path of virtue.

**41.** In this connection it is sufficient briefly to recall to mind examples from history. We shall mention events and facts that admit of no doubt, namely, that human society in its civil aspects was renewed fundamentally by Christian institutions; that, by virtue of this renewal, mankind was raised to a higher level, nay, was called back from death to life, and enriched with such a degree of perfection as had never existed before and was not destined to be greater in any succeeding age; and that, finally, the same Jesus Christ is the beginning and the end of these benefits; for as all things have proceeded from him, so they must be referred back to him. When, with the acceptance of the light of the Gospel, the world had learned the great mystery of the Incarnation of the Word and the redemption of man, the life of Jesus Christ, God and man, spread through the nations and imbued them wholly with his doctrine, with his precepts, and with his laws. Wherefore, if human society is to be healed, only a return to Christian life and institutions will heal it. In the case of decaying societies it is most correctly prescribed that, if they wish to be regenerated, they must be recalled to their origins. For the perfection of all associations is this, namely, to work for and to attain the purpose for which they were formed, so that all social actions should be inspired by the same principle which brought the society itself into being. Wherefore, turning away from the original purpose is corruption, while going back to this purpose is recovery, and just as we affirm this as unquestionably true of the entire body of the commonwealth, in like manner we affirm it of that order of citizens who sustain life by labor and who constitute the vast majority of society.

**42.** But it must not be supposed that the Church so concentrates her energies on caring for souls as to overlook things which pertain to mortal and earthly life. As regards the nonowning workers specifically, she desires and strives that they rise from their most wretched state and enjoy better conditions. And to achieve this result she makes no small contribution by the very fact that she calls men to and trains them in virtue. For when Christian morals are completely observed, they yield of themselves a certain measure of prosperity to material

27

existence, because they win the favor of God, the source and fountain of all goods; because they restrain the twin plagues of life—excessive desire for wealth and thirst[23] for pleasure—which too often make man wretched amidst the very abundance of riches; and because finally, Christian morals make men content with a moderate livelihood and make them supplement income by thrift, removing them far from the vices which swallow up both modest sums and huge fortunes, and dissipate splendid inheritances.

**43.** But, in addition, the Church provides directly for the well-being of the nonowning workers by instituting and promoting activities which she knows to be suitable to relieve their distress. Nay, even in the field of works of mercy, she has always so excelled that she is highly praised by her very enemies. The force of mutual charity among the first Christians was such that the wealthier very often divested themselves of their riches to aid others; wherefore: "Nor was there anyone among them in want."[24] To the deacons, an order founded expressly for this purpose, the apostles assigned the duty of dispensing alms daily; and the apostle Paul, although burdened with the care of all the churches, did not hesitate to spend himself on toilsome journeys in order to bring alms personally to the poorer Christians. Monies of this kind, contributed voluntarily by the Christians in every assembly, Tertullian calls "piety's deposit fund," because they were expended to "support and bury poor people, to supply the wants of orphan boys and girls without means of support, of aged household servants, and of such, too, as had suffered shipwreck."[25]

**44.** Thence, gradually there came into existence that patrimony which the Church has guarded with religious care as the property of the poor. Nay, even disregarding the feeling of shame associated with begging, she provided aid for the wretched poor. For, as the common parent of rich and poor, with charity everywhere stimulated to the highest degree, she founded religious societies and numerous other useful bodies, so that, with the aid which these furnished, there was scarcely any form of human misery that went uncared for.

**45.** And yet many today go so far as to condemn the Church as the ancient pagans once did, for such outstanding charity, and would substitute in lieu thereof a system of benevolence established by the laws of the state. But no human devices can ever be found to supplant Christian charity, which gives itself entirely for the benefit of others. This virtue belongs to the Church alone, for, unless it is derived from the Most Sacred Heart of Jesus, it is in no wise a virtue; and whosoever departs from the Church wanders far from Christ.

---

[23] Cf. 1 Tm 6:10.
[24] Acts 4:34.
[25] *Apol. II*, 39.

**46.** But there can be no question that, to attain our purpose, those helps also which are within the power of men are necessary. Absolutely all who are concerned with the matter must, according to their capacity, bend their efforts to this same end and work for it. And this activity has a certain likeness to Divine Providence governing the world; for generally we see effects flow from the concert of all the elements upon which as causes these effects depend.

**47.** But it is now in order to inquire what portion of the remedy should be expected from the state. By state here we understand not the form of government which this or that people has, but rather that form which right reason in accordance with nature requires and the teachings of divine wisdom approve, matters that we have explained specifically in our encyclical *On the Christian Constitution of States*.

**48.** Therefore those governing the state ought primarily to devote themselves to the service of individual groups and of the whole commonwealth, and through the entire scheme of laws and institutions to cause both public and individual well-being to develop spontaneously out of the very structure and administration of the state. For this is the duty of wise statesmanship and the essential office of those in charge of the state. Now, states are made prosperous especially by wholesome morality, properly ordered family life, protection of religion and justice, moderate imposition and equitable distribution of public burdens, progressive development of industry and trade, thriving agriculture, and by all other things of this nature, which the more actively they are promoted, the better and happier the life of the citizens is destined to be. Therefore, by virtue of these things, it is within the competence of the rulers of the state that, as they benefit other groups, they also improve in particular the condition of the workers. Furthermore, they do this with full right and without laying themselves open to any charge of unwarranted interference. For the state is bound by the very law of its office to serve the common interest. And the richer the benefits which come from this general providence on the part of the state, the less necessary it will be to experiment with other measures for the well-being of workers.

**49.** This ought to be considered, as it touches the question more deeply, namely, that the state has one basic purpose for existence, which embraces in common the highest and the lowest of its members. Nonowning workers are unquestionably citizens by nature in virtue of the same right as the rich, that is, true and vital parts whence, through the medium of families, the body of the state is constituted; and it hardly need be added that they are by far the greatest number in every urban area. Since it would be quite absurd to look out for one portion of the citizens and to neglect another, it follows that public authority ought to exercise due care in safeguarding the well-being and the interests of nonowning workers. Unless this is done, justice, which commands that everyone be given his own, will be violated. Wherefore St. Thomas says wisely: "Even as part and whole are in a certain way the same, so too that which pertains to the whole pertains in a certain way to the part also."[26] Consequently, among the numerous and weighty duties of rulers who would serve their people well, this is first and foremost, namely, that they protect equitably each and every class of citizens, maintaining inviolate that justice especially which is called *distributive*.

50. Although all citizens, without exception, are obliged to contribute something to the sum total common goods, some share of which naturally goes back to each individual, yet all can by no means contribute the same amount and in equal degree. Whatever the vicissitudes that occur in the forms of government, there will always be those differences in the condition of citizens without which society could neither exist nor be conceived. It is altogether necessary that there be some who dedicate themselves to the service of the state, who make laws, who dispense justice, and finally, by whose counsel and authority civil and military affairs are administered. These men, as is clear, play the chief role in the state, and among every people are to be regarded as occupying first place, because they work for the common good most directly and preeminently. On the other hand, those engaged in some calling benefit the state, but not in the same way as the men just mentioned, nor by performing the same duties; yet they, too, in a high degree, although less directly, serve the public weal. Assuredly, since social good must be of such a character that men through its acquisition are made better, it must necessarily be founded chiefly on virtue.

51. Nevertheless, an abundance of corporeal and external goods is likewise a characteristic of a well constituted state, "the use of which goods is necessary for the practice of virtue."[27] To produce these goods the labor of the workers, whether they expend their skill and strength on farms or in factories, is most efficacious and necessary. Nay, in this respect, their energy and effectiveness are so important that it is incontestable that the wealth of nations originates from no other source than from the labor of workers. Equity therefore commands that public authority show proper concern for the worker so that from what he contributes to the common good he may receive what will enable him, housed, clothed, and secure, to live his life without hardship. Whence, it follows that all those measures ought to be favored which seem in any way capable of benefiting the condition of workers. Such solicitude is so far from injuring anyone, that it is destined rather to benefit all, because it is of absolute interest to

---

[26] *Summa theologica*, II-II, Q. 61, Art. 1 and 2.
[27] St. Thomas, *De regimine principum*, I, 15.

the state that those citizens should not be miserable in every respect from whom such necessary goods proceed.

**52.** It is not right, as we have said, for either the citizen or the family to be absorbed by the state; it is proper that the individual and the family should be permitted to retain their freedom of action, so far as this is possible without jeopardizing the common good and without injuring anyone. Nevertheless, those who govern must see to it that they protect the community and its constituent parts: the community, because nature has entrusted its safeguarding to the sovereign power in the state to such an extent that the protection of the public welfare is not only the supreme law, but is the entire cause and reason for sovereignty; and the constituent parts, because philosophy and Christian faith agree that the administration of the state has from nature as its purpose, not the benefit of those to whom it has been entrusted, but the benefit of those who have been entrusted to it. And since the power of governing comes from God and is a participation, as it were, in his supreme sovereignty, it ought to be administered according to the example of the divine power, which looks with paternal care to the welfare of individual creatures as well as to that of all creation. If, therefore, any injury has been done to or threatens either the common good or the interests of individual groups, which injury cannot in any other way be repaired or prevented, it is necessary for public authority to intervene.

**53.** It is vitally important to public as well as to private welfare that there be peace and good order; likewise, that the whole regime of family life be directed according to the ordinances of God and the principles of nature, that religion be observed and cultivated, that sound morals flourish in private and public life, that justice be kept sacred and that no one be wronged with impunity by another, and that strong citizens grow up, capable of supporting, and, if necessary, of protecting the state. Wherefore, if at any time disorder should threaten because of strikes or concerted stoppages of work, if the natural bonds of family life should be relaxed among the poor, if religion among the workers should be outraged by failure to provide sufficient opportunity for performing religious duties, if in factories danger should assail the integrity of morals through the mixing of the sexes or other pernicious incitements to sin, or if the employer class should oppress the working class with unjust burdens or should degrade them with conditions inimical to human personality or to human dignity, if health should be injured by immoderate work and such as is not suited to sex or age—in all these cases, the power and authority of the law, but of course within certain limits, manifestly ought to be employed. And these limits are determined by the same reason which demands the aid of the law, that is, the law ought not undertake more, nor it go farther, than the remedy of evils or the removal of danger requires.

**54.** Rights indeed, by whomsoever possessed, must be religiously protected; and public authority, in warding off injuries and punishing wrongs, ought to see to it that individuals may have and hold what belongs to them. In protecting the rights of private individuals, however, special consideration must be given to the weak and the poor. For the nation, as it were, of the rich, is guarded by its own defenses and is in less need of governmental protection, whereas the suffering multitude, without the means to protect itself, relies especially on the protection of the state. Wherefore, since wage workers are numbered among the great mass of the needy, the state must include them under its special care and foresight.

**55.** But it will be well to touch here expressly on certain matters of special importance. The capital point is this, that private property ought to be safeguarded by the sovereign power of the state and through the bulwark of its laws. And especially, in view of such a great flaming up of passion at the present time, the masses ought to be kept within the bounds of their moral obligations. For while justice does not oppose our striving for better things, on the other hand, it does forbid anyone to take from another what is his and, in the name of a certain absurd equality, to seize forcibly the property of others; nor does the interest of the common good itself permit this. Certainly, the great majority of working people prefer to secure better conditions by honest toil, without doing wrong to anyone. Nevertheless, not a few individuals are found who, imbued with evil ideas and eager for revolution, use every means to stir up disorder and incite to violence. The authority of the state, therefore, should intervene and, by putting restraint upon such disturbers, protect the morals of workers from their corrupting arts and lawful owners from the danger of spoliation.

**56.** Labor which is too long and too hard and the belief that pay is inadequate not infrequently give workers cause to strike and become voluntarily idle. This evil, which is frequent and serious, ought to be remedied by public authority, because such interruption of work inflicts damage not only upon employers and upon the workers themselves, but also injures trade and commerce and the general interests of the state; and, since it is usually not far removed from violence and rioting, it very frequently jeopardizes public peace. In this matter it is more effective and salutary that the authority of the law anticipate and completely prevent the evil from breaking out by removing early the causes from which it would seem that conflict between employers and workers is bound to arise.

**57.** And in like manner, in the case of the worker, there are many things which the power of the state should protect; and, first of all, the goods of his soul. For however good and desirable mortal life be, yet it is not the ultimate goal for which we are born, but a road only and a means for perfecting, through knowledge of truth and love of good, the life of the soul. The soul bears the express image and likeness of God, and there resides in it that sovereignty through the medium of which man has been bidden to rule all created nature below him and to make all lands and all seas serve his interests. "Fill the earth and subdue it, and rule over the fishes of the sea and the fowls of the air and all living creatures that move upon the earth."[28] In this respect all men are equal, and there is no difference between rich and poor, between masters and servants, between rulers and subjects: "For there is the same Lord of all."[29] No one may with impunity outrage the dignity of man, which God himself treats with great reverence, nor impede his course to that level of perfection which accords with eternal life in heaven. Nay, more, in this connection a man cannot even by his own free choice allow himself to be treated in a way inconsistent with his nature, and suffer his soul to be enslaved; for there is no question here of rights belonging to man, but of duties owed to God, which are to be religiously observed.

**58.** Hence follows necessary cessation from toil and work on Sundays and Holy Days of Obligation. Let no one, however, understand this in the sense of greater indulgence of idle leisure, and much less in the sense of that kind of cessation from work, such as many desire, which encourages vice and promotes wasteful spending of money, but solely in the sense of a repose from labor made sacred by religion. Rest combined with religion calls man away from toil and the business of daily life to admonish him to ponder on heavenly goods and to pay his just and due homage to the Eternal Diety. This is especially the nature, and this the cause, of the rest to be taken on Sundays and Holy Days of Obligation, and God has sanctioned the same in the Old Testament by a special law: "Remember thou keep holy the Sabbath Day,"[30] and he himself taught it by his own action: namely the mystical rest taken immediately after he had created man: "He rested on the seventh day from all his work which he had done."[31]

**59.** Now as concerns the protection of corporeal and physical goods, the oppressed workers, above all, ought to be liberated from the savagery of greedy men, who inordinately use human beings as things for gain. Assuredly, neither justice nor humanity can countenance the exaction of so much work that the spirit is dulled from excessive toil and that along with it the body sinks crushed from exhaustion. The working energy of a man, like his entire nature, is circumscribed by definite limits beyond which it cannot go. It is developed indeed by exercise and use, but only on condition that a man cease from work at regular intervals and rest. With respect to daily work, there-

---

[28]Gn 1:28.
[29]Rom 10:12.
[30]Ex 20:8.
[31]Gn 2:2.

fore, care ought to be taken not to extend it beyond the hours that human strength warrants. The length of rest intervals ought to be decided on the basis of the varying nature of the work, of the circumstances of time and place, and of the physical condition of the workers themselves. Since the labor of those who quarry stone from the earth, or who mine iron, copper, and other underground materials, is much more severe and harmful to health, the working period for such men ought to be correspondingly shortened. The seasons of the year also must be taken into account; for often a given kind of work is easy to endure in one season but cannot be endured at all in another, or not without the greatest difficulty.

60. Finally, it is not right to demand of a woman or a child what a strong adult man is capable of doing or would be willing to do. Nay, as regards children, special care ought to be taken that the factory does not get hold of them before age has sufficiently matured their physical, intellectual, and moral powers. For budding strength in childhood, like greening verdure in spring, is crushed by premature harsh treatment; and under such circumstances all education of the child must needs be foregone. Certain occupations likewise are less fitted for women, who are intended by nature for work of the home—work indeed which especially protects modesty in women and accords by nature with the education of children and the well-being of the family. Let it be the rule everywhere that workers be given as much leisure as will compensate for the energy consumed by toil, for rest from work is necessary to restore strength consumed by use. In every obligation which is mutually contracted between employers and workers, this condition, either written or tacit, is always present, that both kinds of rest be provided for; nor would it be equitable to make an agreement otherwise, because no one has the right to demand of, or to make an agreement with anyone to neglect those duties which bind a man to God or to himself.

61. We shall now touch upon a matter of very great importance, and one which must be correctly understood in order to avoid falling into error on one side or the other. We are told that free consent fixes the amount of a wage; that therefore the employer, after paying the wage agreed to would seem to have discharged his obligation and not to owe anything more; that only then would injustice be done if either the employer should refuse to pay the whole amount of the wage, or the worker should refuse to perform all the work to which he had committed himself; and that in these cases, but in no others, is it proper for the public authority to intervene to safeguard the rights of each party.

62. An impartial judge would not assent readily or without reservation to this reasoning, because it is not complete in all respects; one factor to be considered, and one of the greatest importance, is missing. To work is to expend one's energy for the purpose of secur-

ing the things necessary for the various needs of life and especially for its preservation. "In the sweat of thy face shalt thou eat bread."[32] Accordingly, in man labor has two marks, as it were, implanted by nature, so that it is truly *personal*, because work energy inheres in the person and belongs completely to him by whom it is expended and for whose use it is destined by nature; and, secondly, that it is *necessary*, because man has need of the fruit of his labors to preserve his life, and nature itself, which must be most strictly obeyed, commands him to preserve it. If labor should be considered only under the aspect that it is personal, there is no doubt that it would be entirely in the worker's power to set the amount of the agreed wage at too low a figure. For inasmuch as he performs work by his own free will, he can also by his own free will be satisfied with either a paltry wage for his work or even with none at all. But this matter must be judged far differently, if with the factor of *personality* we combine the factor of *necessity*, from which indeed the former is separable in thought but not in reality. In fact, to preserve one's life is a duty common to all individuals, and to neglect this duty is a crime. Hence arises necessarily the right of securing things to sustain life, and only a wage earned by his labor gives a poor man the means to acquire these things.

**63.** Let it be granted then that worker and employer may enter freely into agreements and, in particular, concerning the amount of the wage; yet there is always underlying such agreements an element of natural justice, and one greater and more ancient than the free consent of contracting parties, namely, that the wage shall not be less than enough to support a worker who is thrifty and upright. If, compelled by necessity or moved by fear of a worse evil, a worker accepts a harder condition, which although against his will he must accept because the employer or contractor imposes it, he certainly submits to force, against which justice cries out in protest.

**64.** But in these and similar questions, such as the number of hours of work in each kind of occupation and the health safeguards to be provided, particularly in factories, it will be better, in order to avoid unwarranted governmental intervention, especially since circumstances of business, season, and place are so varied, that decision be reserved to the organizations of which we are about to speak below, or else to pursue another course whereby the interests of the workers may be adequately safeguarded—the state, if the occasion demands, to furnish help and protection.

**65.** If a worker receives a wage sufficiently large to enable him to provide comfortably for himself, his wife and his children, he will, if prudent, gladly strive to practice thrift; and the result will be, as

---

[32]Gn 3:19.

35

nature itself seems to counsel, that after expenditures are deducted there will remain something over and above through which he can come into the possession of a little wealth. We have seen, in fact, that the whole question under consideration cannot be settled effectually unless it is assumed and established as a principle, that the right of private property must be regarded as sacred. Wherefore, the law ought to favor this right and, so far as it can, see that the largest possible number among the masses of the population prefer to own property.

66. If this is done, excellent benefits will follow, foremost among which will surely be a more equitable division of goods. For the violence of public disorder has divided cities into two classes of citizens, with an immense gulf lying between them. On the one side is a faction exceedingly powerful because exceedingly rich. Since it alone has under its control every kind of work and business, it diverts to its own advantage and interest all production sources of wealth and exerts no little power in the administration itself of the state. On the other side are the needy and helpless masses, with minds inflamed and always ready for disorder. But if the productive activity of the multitude can be stimulated by the hope of acquiring some property in land, it will gradually come to pass that, with the difference between extreme wealth and extreme penury removed, one class will become neighbor to the other. Moreover, there will surely be a greater abundance of the things which the earth produces. For when men know they are working on what belongs to them, they work with far greater eagerness and diligence. Nay, in a word, they learn to love the land cultivated by their own hands, whence they look not only for food but for some measure of abundance for themselves and their dependents. All can see how much this willing eagerness contributes to an abundance of produce and the wealth of a nation. Hence, in the third place, will flow the benefit that men can easily be kept from leaving the country in which they have been born and bred; for they would not exchange their native country for a foreign land if their native country furnished them sufficient means of living.

67. But these advantages can be attained only if private wealth is not drained away by crushing taxes of every kind. For since the right of possessing goods privately has been conferred not by man's law, but by nature, public authority cannot abolish it, but can only control its exercise and bring it into conformity with the commonweal. Public authority therefore would act unjustly and inhumanly, if in the name of taxes it should appropriate from the property of private individuals more than is equitable.

68. Finally, employers and workers themselves can accomplish much in this matter, manifestly through those institutions by the help of which the poor are opportunely assisted and the two classes of society are brought closer to each other. Under this category come associa-

tions for giving mutual aid; various agencies established by the foresight of private persons to care for the worker and likewise for his dependent wife and children in the event that an accident, sickness, or death befalls him; and foundations to care for boys and girls, for adolescents, and for the aged.

**69.** But associations of workers occupy first place, and they include within their circle nearly all the rest. The beneficent achievements of the guilds of artisans among our ancestors have long been well known. Truly, they yielded noteworthy advantages not only to artisans, but, as many monuments bear witness, brought glory and progress to the arts themselves. In our present age of greater culture, with its new customs and ways of living, and with the increased number of things required by daily life, it is most clearly necessary that workers' associations be adapted to meet the present need. It is gratifying that societies of this kind composed either of workers alone or of workers and employers together are being formed everywhere, and it is truly to be desired that they grow in number and in active vigor. Although we have spoken of them more than once, it seems well to show in this place that they are highly opportune and are formed by their own right, and, likewise to show how they should be organized and what they should do.

**70.** Inadequacy of his own strength, learned from experience, impels and urges a man to enlist the help of others. Such is the teaching of Holy Scripture: "It is better therefore that two should be together, than one: for they have the advantage of their society. If one fall he shall be supported by the other; woe to him that is alone, for when he falleth he hath none to life him up."[33] And this also: "A brother that is helped by his brother, is like a strong city."[34] Just as man is drawn by this natural propensity into civil union and association, so also he seeks with his fellow citizens to form other societies, admittedly small and not perfect, but societies nonetheless.

**71.** Between these latter and the large society of the state, there is, because of their different immediate purposes, a very great distinction. The end of civil society concerns absolutely all members of this society, since the end of civil society is centered in the common good, in which latter, one and all in due proportion have a right to participate. Wherefore, this society is called *public*, because through it "men share with one another in establishing a commonwealth."[35] On the other hand, societies which are formed, so to speak, within its bosom are considered *private* and are such because their immediate object is private advantage, appertaining to those alone who are thus associ-

---

[33]Eccl 4:9-10.
[34]Prv 18:19.
[35]St.Thomas, *Contra impugnantes Dei cultum et religionem* II, 8.

ated together. "Now a private society is one which is formed to carry out some private business, as when two or three enter into association for the purpose of engaging together in trade."[36]

72. Although private societies exist within the state and are, as it were, so many parts of it, still it is not within the authority of the state universally and *per se* to forbid them to exist as such. For man is permitted by a right of nature to form private societies; the state, on the other hand, has been instituted to protect and not to destroy natural right, and if it should forbid its citizens to enter into associations, it would clearly do something contradictory to itself because both the state itself and private associations are begotten of one and the same principle, namely, that men are by nature inclined to associate. Occasionally there are times when it is proper for the laws to oppose associations of this kind, that is, if they professedly seek after any objective which is clearly at variance with good morals, with justice or with the welfare of the state. Indeed, in these cases the public power shall justly prevent such associations from forming and shall also justly dissolve those already formed. Nevertheless, it must use the greatest precaution lest it appear to infringe on the rights of its citizens, and lest, under the pretext of public benefit it enact any measure that sound reason would not support. For laws are to be obeyed only insofar as they conform with right reason and thus with the external law of God.[37]

73. Here come to our mind for consideration the various confraternities, societies, and religious orders which the authority of the Church and the piety of Christians have brought into being; and history down to our own times speaks of the wonderful benefit they have been to the human race. Since societies of this character, even if judged in the light of reason alone, have been formed for an honest purpose, it is clear that they have been formed in accordance with natural right. But in whatever respect they concern religion, they are properly subject to the Church alone. Therefore those in charge of the state cannot in justice arrogate to themselves any right over them or assume their administration to themselves. Rather it is the office of the state to respect, to conserve, and as occasion may require, to protect them from injustice. Yet we have seen something entirely different being done, especially at the present time. In many places the state has violated associations of this kind, and in fact with manifold injury, since it has put them in the bonds of the civil law, has divested them

---

[36]Ibid.
[37]"Human law has the essential nature of law only insofar as it is in accordance with right reason, and thus manifestly it derives from the eternal law. But insofar as it deviates from reason, it is called unjust law, and so it does not have the essential nature of law, but rather of a kind of violence." (St. Thomas, *Summa theologica*, I-II, Q. 93, Art. 3 ad 2.)

of their lawful right to be considered legal persons, and has robbed them of their property. In this property the Church possessed her rights, and individual association members possessed theirs, as did also the persons who donated this property for a designated purpose as well as those for whose benefit and relief it had been donated. Consequently, we cannot refrain from deploring such vicious and unjust acts of robbery, and so much the more because we see the road being closed to Catholic associations, which are law-abiding and in every respect useful, at the very time when it is being decreed that most assuredly men are permitted by law to form associations, and at the very time when this freedom is being lavishly granted in actual fact to men urging courses of conduct pernicious at once to religion and to the state.

74. Certainly, the number of associations of almost every possible kind, especially of associations of workers, is now far greater than ever before. This is not the place to inquire whence many of them originate, what object they have, or how they proceed. But the opinion is, and it is one confirmed by a good deal of evidence, that they are largely under the control of secret leaders and that these leaders apply principles which are in harmony with neither Christianity nor the welfare of states, and that, after having possession of all available work, they contrive that those who refuse to join with them will be forced by want to pay the penalty. Under these circumstances, workers who are Christians must choose one of two things; either to join associations in which it is greatly to be feared that there is danger to religion, or to form their own associations and unite their forces in such a way that they may be able manfully to free themselves from such unjust and intolerable oppression. Can they who refuse to place man's highest good in imminent jeopardy hesitate to affirm that the second course is by all means to be followed?

75. Many of our Faith are indeed to be highly commended, who, having rightly perceived what the times require of them, are experimenting and striving to discover how by honest means they can raise the nonowning working class to higher living levels. They have championed their cause and are endeavoring to increase the prosperity of both families and individuals, and at the same time to regulate justly the mutual obligations which rest upon workers and employers and to foster and strengthen in both consciousness of duty and observance of the precepts of the Gospel—precepts, in truth, which hold man back from excess and prevent him from overstepping the bounds of moderation and, in the midst of the widest divergences among persons and things, maintain harmony in the state. For this reason, we see eminent men meeting together frequently to exchange ideas, to combine their forces, and to deliberate on the most expedient programs of action. Others are endeavoring to unite the various kinds of workers in suitable associations, are assisting them with advice

and money, and making plans to prevent a lack of honest and profitable work. The bishops are giving encouragement and bestowing support; and under their authority and auspices many from the ranks of the clergy, both regular and diocesan, are showing zealous care for all that pertains to the spiritual improvement of the members of these associations. Finally, there are not wanting Catholics of great wealth, yet voluntary sharers, as it were, in the lot of the wage workers, who by their own generous contributions are striving to found and extend associations through which the worker is readily enabled to obtain from his toil not only immediate benefits, but also assurance of honorable retirement in the future. How much good such manifold and enthusiastic activity has contributed to the benefit of all is too well known to make discussion necessary. From all this, we have taken auguries of good hope for the future, provided that societies of this kind continually grow and that they are founded with wise organization. Let the state protect these lawfully associated bodies of citizens; let it not, however, interfere with their private concerns and order of life; for vital activity is set in motion by an inner principle, and it is very easily destroyed, as we know, by intrusion from without.

76. Unquestionably, wise direction and organization are essential to these associations in order that in their activities there be unity of purpose and concord of wills. Furthermore, if citizens have free right to associate, as in fact they do, they also must have the right freely to adopt the organization and the rules which they judge most appropriate to achieve their purpose. We do not feel that the precise character in all details which the aforementioned direction and organization of associations ought to have can be determined by fast and fixed rules, since this is a matter to be decided rather in the light of the temperament of each people, of experiment and practice, of the nature and character of the work, of the extent of trade and commerce, and of other circumstances of a material and temporal kind, all of which must be carefully considered. In summary, let this be laid down as a general and constant law: Workers' associations ought to be so constituted and so governed as to furnish the most suitable and most convenient means to attain the object proposed, which consists in this, that the individual members of the association secure, so far as possible, an increase in the goods of body, of soul, and of prosperity.

77. It is clear, however, that moral and religious perfection ought to be regarded as their principal goal, and that their social organization as such ought above all to be directed completely by this goal. For otherwise they would degenerate in nature and would be little better than those associations in which no account is ordinarily taken of religion. Besides, what would it profit a worker to secure through an association an abundance of goods, if his soul through lack of its

proper food should run the risk of perishing? "What doth it profit a man, if he gain the whole world, but suffer the loss of his own soul?"[38] Christ Our Lord teaches that this in fact must be considered the mark whereby a Christian is distinguished from a pagan: "After all these things the Gentiles seek—seek ye first the kingdom of God and his justice, and all these things shall be given you besides."[39] Therefore, having taken their principles from God, let those associations provide ample opportunity for religious instruction so that individual members may understand their duties to God, that they may well know what to believe, what to hope for, and what to do for eternal salvation, and that with special care they may be fortified against erroneous opinions and various forms of corruption. Let the worker be exhorted to the worship of God and the pursuit of piety, especially to religious observance of Sundays and Holy Days. Let him learn to reverence and love the Church, the common Mother of all, and likewise to observe her precepts and to frequent her Sacraments, which are the divine means for purifying the soul from the stains of sin and for attaining sanctity.

**78.** When the regulations of associations are founded upon religion, the way is easy toward establishing the mutual relations of the members so that peaceful living together and prosperity will result. Offices in the associations are to be distributed properly in accordance with the common interest, and in such a way, moreover, that wide difference in these offices may not create discord. It is of special importance that obligations be apportioned wisely and be clearly defined, to the end that no one is done an injustice. Let the funds be disbursed equitably in such way that the amount of benefit to be paid out to members is fixed beforehand in accordance with individual needs, and let the rights and duties of employers be properly adjusted to the rights and duties of workers. If any one in these two groups feels that he has been injured in any way, nothing is more to be desired than that prudent and upright men of the same body be available, and that the association regulations themselves prescribe that the dispute be settled according to the decision of these men.

**79.** It must also be specially provided that the worker at no time be without sufficient work, and that the monies paid into the treasury of the association furnish the means of assisting individual members in need, not only during sudden and unforeseen changes in industry, but also whenever anyone is stricken by sickness, by old age, or by misfortune.

**80.** Through these regulations, provided they are readily accepted, the interests and welfare of the poor will be adequately cared for.

---

[38]Mt 16:26.
[39]Mt 6:32-33.

Associations of Catholics, moreover, will undoubtedly be of great importance in promoting prosperity in the state. Through past events we can, without temerity, foresee the future. Age presses hard upon age, but there are wondrous similarities in history, governed as it is by the Providence of God, who guides and directs the continuity and the chain of events in accordance with that purpose which he set before himself in creating the human race. In the early ages, when the Church was in her youth, we know that the reproach was hurled at the Christians that the great majority of them lived by precarious alms or by toil. Yet, although destitute of wealth and power, they succeeded in winning the good will of the rich and the protection of the mighty. All could see that they were energetic, industrious, peace-loving, and exemplarily devoted to the practice of justice and especially of charity. In the presence of life and conduct such as this, all prejudice vanished, the taunting voices of the malevolent were silenced, and the falsehoods of inveterate superstition yielded little by little to Christian truth.

81. The condition of workers is a subject of bitter controversy at the present time; and whether this controversy is resolved in accordance with reason or otherwise, is in either event of utmost importance to the state. But Christian workers will readily resolve it in accordance with reason, if, united in associations and under wise leaders, they enter upon the path which their fathers and their ancestors followed to their own best welfare as well as to that of the state. For, no matter how strong the power of prejudice and passion in man, yet, unless perversity of will has deadened the sense of the right and just, the good will of citizens is certain to be more freely inclined toward those whom they learn to know as industrious and temperate, and who clearly place justice before profit and conscientious observance of duty before all else. Under these circumstances there will follow also this great advantage, that no little hope and opportunity for developing a sound attitude will be afforded those workers who live in complete disdain of the Christian Faith or in a manner foreign to its profession. These men indeed, for the most part, know that they have been deceived by illusory hopes and by false appearances. They are conscious of being most inhumanly treated by greedy employers, that almost no greater value is being placed on them than the amount of gain they yield by their toil, and that in the associations, moreover, in whose meshes they are caught, there exist in place of charity and love, internal dissensions which are the inseparable companions of aggravating and irreligious poverty. Broken in spirit, and worn out in body, how gladly many would free themselves from a servitude so degrading! Yet they dare not because either human shame or the fear of want prevents them. It is remarkable how much associations of Catholics can contribute to the welfare of all such men if they invite those wavering in uncertainty to their bosom in order to remedy their

difficulties, and if they receive the penitents into their trust and protection.

**82.** These, venerable brethren, are the persons, and this is the procedure to be employed in dealing with this most difficult question. Everyone according to his position ought to gird himself for the task, and indeed as speedily as possible, lest, by delaying the remedy, the evil, which is already of vast dimensions, become incurable. Let those in charge of states make use of the provision afforded by laws and institutions; let the rich and employers be mindful of their duties; let the workers, whose cause is at stake, press their claims with reason. And since religion alone, as we said in the beginning, can remove the evil, root and branch, let all reflect upon this: First and foremost Christian morals must be reestablished, without which even the weapons of prudence, which are considered especially effective, will be of no avail to secure well-being.

**83.** So far as the Church is concerned, at no time and in no manner will she permit her efforts to be wanting, and she will contribute all the more help in proportion as she has more freedom of action. Let this be understood in particular by those whose duty it is to promote the public welfare. Let the members of the Sacred Ministry exert all their strength of mind and all their diligence, and venerable brethren, under the guidance of your authority and example, let them not cease to impress upon men of all ranks the principles of Christian living as found in the Gospel; by all means in their power let them strive for the well-being of peoples; and especially let them aim both to preserve in themselves and to arouse in others, in the highest equally as well as in the lowest, the mistress and queen of the virtues, charity. Certainly, the well-being which is so longed for is chiefly to be expected from an abundant outpouring of charity; of Christian charity, we mean, which is in epitome the law of the Gospel, and which, always ready to sacrifice itself for the benefit of others, is man's surest antidote against the insolence of the world and immoderate love of self; the divine office and features of this virtue being described by the apostle Paul in these words: "Charity is patient, is kind . . . is not self-seeking . . . bears with all things . . . endures all things."[40]

**84.** As a pledge of divine favor and as a token of our affection, most lovingly in the Lord we bestow on each of you, venerable brethren, on your clergy and on your people, the Apostolic Blessing.

**85.** Given in Rome, at St. Peter's, the 15th day of May, in the year 1891, the fourteenth of our pontificate.

Leo XIII

---

[40] 1 Cor 13:4-7.

43

# Introduction to
# Quadragesimo Anno

On the fortieth anniversary of *Rerum Novarum*, Pope Pius XI issued the second major social encyclical. *Quadragesimo Anno* repeats many of the themes of Leo XIII: the dignity of labor; the rights of workers to organize and even to participate to some degree in ownership, management and profit; the incompatibility of Christian social teaching with communist or socialist economic philosophies.

Though staying more or less within the lines established by *Rerum Novarum*, the encyclical breaks some new ground. Economic concentration had become far more threatening in 1931 than it was in 1891, and Pius XI addresses it squarely. Too few people are entrusted with making basic economic decisions in our society, he says. This results in policies that favor an increasingly small group. The desire for absolute dominance in the economic sphere has totally corrupted the legitimate desire to turn a profit. The whole economy is ruled by harshness and cruelty, especially toward the poor. The Pope demands that this oppression cease.

*Quadragesimo Anno*'s deep concern about economic concentration led to the introduction of an idea destined to become a centerpiece of subsequent Catholic social thought—the principle of subsidiarity. (Though it has roots in *Rerum Novarum*, Pius XI gave subsidiarity its classic formulation.) The principle holds that it is a serious violation of just social order to allow larger political entities to absorb functions that smaller and lower communities can ably carry out. Subsidiarity assigns to the state the responsibility of assisting in the empowerment of smaller groups. The state must not attempt to destroy these groups nor interfere with their operations. The Pope describes the principle as fixed and unchangeable, permitting no compromise.

The principle was not the product of theological reflection alone. There is little doubt that socialism's championing of state centralization was responsible for the importance subsidiarity assumed in Catholic teaching. Today the principle has become somewhat of an ideological football in discussions of Catholic perspectives on economics.

Some would prefer to replace subsidiarity with the principle of participation. The Church could remain neutral regarding the degree

45

of government intervention, as long as a given political system guarantees a real voice to all its citizens. Pope Paul VI's *Populorum Progressio* seems to lean in this direction. Other commentators strongly assert the principle of subsidiarity in defense of an unrestrained form of capitalism, using it as justification for keeping the state from controlling basic economic dynamics. Still others take the middle ground, emphasizing the central place of subsidiarity but rejecting any interpretation of it that glorifies voluntary associations over state institutions or implies unconditionally that "that government governs best which governs least."

Those who adopt this last perspective believe that the term "subsidiarity" must be more precisely defined. As used by Pius XI and his followers, they say, subsidiarity was never intended as a description of the state itself, but rather as a description of how the state ought to relate to freely associated groups devoted to human welfare. The proper Catholic view, according to this line of interpretation, understands social function as a cooperative effort of the governmental and private sectors. Neither should be deemed more important in the overall workings of a society.

This internal Catholic discussion of subsidiarity seems to be far from resolved. Without question it will continue unabated in the future.

# Quadragesimo Anno
## On Reconstructing the Social Order
### POPE PIUS XI

*May 15, 1931*

*To Our Venerable Brethren, the Patriarchs, Primates, Archbishops, Bishops and Other Ordinaries, in Peace and Communion with the Holy See, and Likewise to All the Faithful of the Catholic World: On Reconstructing Social Order and on Perfecting It in Conformity with the Law of the Gospel, in Honor of the Fortieth Anniversary of the Encyclical of Leo XIII, On the Condition of Workers*

Venerable Brethren and Beloved Children
Health and Apostolic Benediction
1.  Forty years have passed since Leo XIII's peerless encyclical, *On the Condition of Workers*, first saw the light, and the whole Catholic world, filled with grateful recollection, is undertaking to commemorate it with befitting solemnity.
2.  Other encyclicals of our predecessor had in a way prepared the path for that outstanding document and proof of pastoral care: namely, those on the family and the Holy Sacrament of Matrimony as the source of human society,[1] on the origin of civil authority[2] and its proper relations with the Church,[3] on the chief duties of Christian citizens,[4] against the tenets of Socialism,[5] against false teachings on human liberty,[6] and others of the same nature fully expressing the mind of Leo XIII. Yet the encyclical, *On the Condition of Workers*, compared with the rest had this special distinction that at a time when it was most opportune and actually necessary to do so, it laid down for all mankind the surest rules to solve aright that difficult problem of human relations called "the social question."

---

[1] Encyclical, *Arcanum*, Feb. 10, 1880.
[2] Encyclical, *Diuturnum*, June 20, 1881.
[3] Encyclical, *Immortale Dei*, Nov. 1, 1885.
[4] Encyclical, *Sapientiae Christianae*, Jan. 10, 1890.
[5] Encyclical, *Quod Apostolici Muneris*, Dec. 28, 1878.
[6] Encyclical, *Libertas*, June 20, 1888.

# The Occasion

**3.** For toward the close of the nineteenth century, the new kind of economic life that had arisen and the new developments of industry had gone to the point in most countries that human society was clearly becoming divided more and more into two classes. One class, very small in number, was enjoying almost all the advantages which modern inventions so abundantly provided; the other, embracing the huge multitude of working people, oppressed by wretched poverty, was vainly seeking escape from the straits wherein it stood.

**4.** Quite agreeable, of course, was this state of things to those who thought it in their abundant riches the result of inevitable economic laws and accordingly, as if it were for charity to veil the violation of justice which lawmakers not only tolerated but at times sanctioned, wanted the whole care of supporting the poor committed to charity alone. The workers, on the other hand, crushed by their hard lot, were barely enduring it and were refusing longer to bend their necks beneath so galling a yoke; and some of them, carried away by the heat of evil counsel, were seeking the overturn of everything, while others, whom Christian training restrained from such evil designs, stood firm in the judgment that much in this had to be wholly and speedily changed.

**5.** The same feeling those many Catholics, both priests and laymen, shared, whom a truly wonderful charity had long spurred on to relieve the unmerited poverty of the nonowning workers, and who could in no way convince themselves that so enormous and unjust an inequality in the distribution of this world's goods truly conforms to the designs of the all-wise Creator.

**6.** Those men were without question sincerely seeking an immediate remedy for this lamentable disorganization of states and a secure safeguard against worse dangers. Yet such is the weakness of even the best of human minds that, now rejected as dangerous innovators, now hindered in the good work by their very associates advocating other courses of action, and, uncertain in the face of various opinions, they were at a loss which way to turn.

**7.** In such a sharp conflict of minds, therefore, while the question at issue was being argued this way and that, nor always with calmness, all eyes as often before turned to the Chair of Peter, to that sacred depository of all truth whence words of salvation pour forth to all the world. And to the feet of Christ's Vicar on earth were flocking in unaccustomed numbers, men well versed in social questions, employers, and workers themselves, begging him with one voice to point out, finally, the safe road to them.

**8.** The wise Pontiff long weighed all this in his mind before God; he summoned the most experienced and learned to counsel; he pondered the issues carefully and from every angle. At last, admonished "by the consciousness of His Apostolic Office"[7] lest silence on his part might be regarded as failure in his duty[8] he decided, in virtue of the Divine Teaching Office entrusted to him, to address not only the whole Church of Christ but all mankind.

9.  Therefore on the fifteenth day of May, 1891, that long awaited voice thundered forth; neither daunted by the arduousness of the problem nor weakened by age with vigorous energy, it taught the whole human family to strike out in the social question upon new paths.

## Chief Headings

10.  You know, venerable brethren and beloved children, and understand full well the wonderful teaching which has made the encyclical, *On the Condition of Workers*, illustrious forever. The Supreme Pastor in this letter, grieving that so large a portion of mankind should "live undeservedly in miserable and wretched conditions,"[9] took it upon himself with great courage to defend "the cause of the workers whom the present age had handed over, each alone and defenseless, to the inhumanity of employers and the unbridled greed of competitors."[10] He sought no help from either Liberalism or Socialism, for the one had proved that it was utterly unable to solve the social problem aright, and the other, proposing a remedy far worse than the evil itself, would have plunged human society into greater dangers.

11.  Since a problem was being treated "for which no satisfactory solution" is found "unless religion and the Church have been called upon to aid,"[11] the pope, clearly exercising his right and correctly holding that the guardianship of religion and the stewardship over those things that are closely bound up with it had been entrusted especially to him and relying solely upon the unchangeable principles drawn from the treasury of right reason and Divine Revelation, confidently and *as one having authority*,[12] declared and proclaimed "the rights and duties within which the rich and proletariat—those who furnish material things and those who furnish work—ought to be restricted in relation to each other,"[13] and what the Church, heads of states and the people themselves directly concerned ought to do.

---

[7]Encyclical, *On the Condition of Workers*, May 15, 1891, § 3.
[8]Ibid. cf. § 24.
[9]Ibid. cf. § 5.
[10]Ibid. cf. § 6.
[11]Ibid. cf. § 24.
[12]Cf. Mt 7:29.
[13]Encyclical, *On the Condition of Workers*, § 4.

**12.** The apostolic voice did not thunder forth in vain. On the contrary, not only did the obedient children of the Church hearken to it with marvelling admiration and hail it with the greatest applause, but many also who were wandering far from the truth, from the unity of the faith, and nearly all who since then either in private study or in enacting legislation have concerned themselves with the social and economic question.

**13.** Feeling themselves vindicated and defended by the Supreme Authority on earth, Christian workers received this encyclical with special joy. So, too, did all those noble-hearted men who, long solicitous for the improvement of the condition of the workers, had up to that time encountered almost nothing but indifference from many, and even rankling suspicion, if not open hostility, from some. Rightly, therefore, have all these groups constantly held the apostolic encyclical from that time in such high honor that to signify their gratitude they are wont, in various places and in various ways, to commemorate it every year.

**14.** However, in spite of such great agreement, there were some who were not a little disturbed; and so it happened that the teaching of Leo XIII, so noble and lofty and so utterly new to worldly ears, was held suspect by some, even among Catholics, and to certain ones it even gave offense. For it boldly attacked and overturned the idols of Liberalism, ignored longstanding prejudices, and was in advance of its time beyond all expectation, so that the slow of heart disdained to study this new social philosophy and the timid feared to scale so lofty a height. There were some also who stood, indeed, in awe at its splendor, but regarded it as a kind of imaginary ideal of perfection more desirable than attainable.

## Scope of the Present Encyclical

**15.** Venerable brethren and beloved children, as all everywhere and especially Catholic workers who are pouring from all sides into this Holy City, are celebrating with such enthusiasm the solemn commemoration of the fortieth anniversary of the encyclical *On the Condition of Workers*, we deem it fitting on this occasion to recall the great benefits this encyclical has brought to the Catholic Church and to all human society; to defend the illustrious Master's doctrine on the social and economic question against certain doubts and to develop it more fully as to some points; and lastly, summoning to court the contemporary economic regime and passing judgment on Socialism, to lay bare the root of the existing social confusion and at the same time point the only way to sound restoration; namely, the Christian reform of morals. All these matters which we undertake to treat will fall under three main headings, and this entire encyclical will be devoted to their development.

---

# I.  Benefits Which Have Come from
## *On the Condition of Workers*

**16.** To begin with the topic which we have proposed first to discuss, we cannot refrain, following the counsel of St. Ambrose[14] who says that "no duty is more important than that of returning thanks," from offering our fullest gratitude to Almighty God for the immense benefits that have come through Leo's encyclical to the Church and to human society. If indeed we should wish to review these benefits even cursorily, almost the whole history of the social question during the last forty years would have to be recalled to mind. These benefits can be reduced conveniently, however, to three main points, corresponding to the three kinds of help which our predecessor ardently desired for the accomplishment of his great work of restoration.

### *1. What the Church Has Done*

**17.** In the first place Leo himself clearly stated what ought to be expected from the Church:

> Manifestly it is the Church which draws from the Gospel the teachings through which the struggle can be composed entirely, or, after its bitterness is removed, can certainly become more tempered. It is the Church, again, that strives not only to instruct the mind, but to regulate by her precepts the life and morals of individuals, and that ameliorates the condition of the workers through her numerous and beneficent institutions.[15]

**In Teachings**

**18.** The Church did not let these rich fountains lie quiescent in her bosom, but from them drew copiously for the common good of the longed-for peace. Leo himself and his successors, showing paternal charity and pastoral constancy always, in defense especially of the poor and the weak,[16] proclaimed and urged without ceasing again

---

[14]St. Ambrose, *De excessu fratris sui Satyri* I. 44.
[15]Encyclical, *On the Condition of Workers*, § 25.
[16]Let it be sufficient to mention some of these only: Leo XIII's apostolic letter *Praeclara*, June 20, 1894, and encyclical *Graves de Communi*, Jan. 18, 1901; Pius X's motu proprio *De Actione Populari Christiana*, Dec. 8, 1903; Benedict XV's encyclical *Ad Beatissimi*, Nov. 1, 1914; Pius IX's encyclical *Ubi Arcano*, Dec. 23, 1922, and encyclical *Rite Expiatis*, Apr. 30, 1926.

and again by voice and pen the teaching on the social and economic question which *On the Condition of Workers* presented, and adapted it fittingly to the needs of time and of circumstance. And many bishops have done the same, who in their continual and able interpretation of this same teaching have illustrated it with commentaries and in accordance with the mind and instructions of the Holy See provided for its application to the conditions and institutions of diverse regions.[17]

**19.** It is not surprising, therefore, that many scholars, both priests and laymen, led especially by the desire that the unchanged and unchangeable teaching of the Church should meet new demands and needs more effectively, have zealously undertaken to develop, with the Church as their guide and teacher, a social and economic science in accord with the conditions of our time.

**20.** And so, with Leo's encyclical pointing the way and furnishing the light, a true Catholic social science has arisen, which is daily fostered and enriched by the tireless efforts of those chosen men whom we have termed auxiliaries of the Church. They do not, indeed, allow their science to lie hidden behind learned walls. As the useful and well attended courses instituted in Catholic universities, colleges, and seminaries, the social congresses and "weeks" that are held at frequent intervals with most successful results, the study groups that are promoted, and finally the timely and sound publications that are disseminated everywhere and in every possible way, clearly show, these men bring their science out into the full light and stress of life.

**21.** Nor is the benefit that has poured forth from Leo's encyclical confined within these bounds; for the teaching which *On the Condition of Workers* contains has gradually and imperceptibly worked its way into the minds of those outside Catholic unity who do not recognize the authority of the Church. Catholic principles on the social question have as a result, passed little by little into the patrimony of all human society, and we rejoice that the eternal truths which our predecessor of glorious memory proclaimed so impressively have been frequently invoked and defended not only in non-Catholic books and journals but in legislative halls also and courts of justice.

**22.** Furthermore, after the terrible war, when the statesmen of the leading nations were attempting to restore peace on the basis of a thorough reform of social conditions, did not they, among the norms agreed upon to regulate in accordance with justice and equity the labor of the workers, give sanction to many points that so remarkably coincide with Leo's principles and instructions as to seem consciously

---

[17]Cf. *La Hiérarchie catholique et le problème social depuis l'Encyclique "Rerum Novarum,"* 1891-1931, pp. XVI-335; ed. "Union internationale d'Etudes sociales fondée à Malines, en 1920, sous la présidence du Card. Mercier." Paris, Éditions "Spes," 1931.

taken therefrom? The encyclical *On the Condition of Workers*, without question, has become a memorable document and rightly to it may be applied the words of Isaiah: "He shall set up a standard to the nations."[18]

## In Applying the Teachings

**23.** Meanwhile, as Leo's teachings were being widely diffused in the minds of men, with learned investigations leading the way, they have come to be put into practice. In the first place, zealous efforts have been made, with active good will, to lift up that class which on account of the modern expansion of industry had increased to enormous numbers but not yet had obtained its rightful place or rank in human society and was, for that reason, all but neglected and despised—the workers, we mean—to whose improvement, to the great advantage of souls, the diocesan and regular clergy, though burdened with other pastoral duties, have under the leadership of the bishops devoted themselves. This constant work, undertaken to fill the workers' souls with the Christian spirit, helped much also to make them conscious of their true dignity and render them capable, by placing clearly before them the rights and duties of their class, of legitimately and happily advancing and even of becoming leaders of their fellows.

**24.** From that time on, fuller means of livelihood have been more securely obtained; for not only did works of beneficence and charity begin to multiply at the urging of the Pontiff, but there have also been established everywhere new and continuously expanding organizations in which workers, craftsmen, farmers, and employees of every kind, with the counsel of the Church and frequently under the leadership of her priests, give and receive mutual help and support.

## 2. What Civil Authority Has Done

**25.** With regard to civil authority, Leo XIII, boldly breaking through the confines imposed by Liberalism, fearlessly taught that government must not be thought a mere guardian of law and of good order, but rather must put forth every effort so that "through the entire scheme of laws and institutions. . . . both public and individual well-being may develop spontaneously out of the very structure and administration of the state."[19] Just freedom of action must, of course, be left both to individual citizens and to families, yet only on condition that the common good be preserved and wrong to any individual be

---

[18]Is 11:12.
[19]Encyclical, *On the Condition of Workers*, § 48.

abolished. The function of the rulers of the state, moreover, is to watch over the community and its parts; but in protecting private individuals in their rights, chief consideration ought to be given to the weak and the poor. "For the nation, as it were, of the rich is guarded by its own defenses and is in less need of governmental protection, whereas the suffering multitude, without the means to protect itself relies especially on the protection of the state. Wherefore, since wage-workers are numbered among the great mass of the needy, the state must include them under its special care and foresight."[20]

**26.** We, of course, do not deny that even before the encyclical of Leo, some rulers of peoples had provided for certain of the more urgent needs of the workers and curbed more flagrant acts of injustice inflicted upon them. But after the apostolic voice had sounded from the Chair of Peter throughout the world, rulers of nations, more fully alive at last to their duty, devoted their minds and attention to the task of promoting a more comprehensive and fruitful social policy.

**27.** And while the principles of Liberalism were tottering, which had long prevented effective action by those governing the state, the encyclical *On the Condition of Workers* in truth impelled peoples themselves to promote a social policy on truer grounds and with greater intensity, and so strongly encouraged good Catholics to furnish valuable help to heads of states in this field that they often stood forth as illustrious champions of this new policy even in legislatures. Sacred ministers of the Church, thoroughly imbued with Leo's teaching, have, in fact, often proposed to the votes of the peoples' representatives the very social legislation that has been enacted in recent years and have resolutely demanded and promoted its enforcement.

**28.** A new branch of law, wholly unknown to the earlier time, has arisen from this continuous and unwearied labor to protect vigorously the sacred rights of the workers that flow from their dignity as men and as Christians. These laws undertake the protection of life, health, strength, family, homes, workshops, wages and labor hazards, in fine, everything which pertains to the conditions of wage workers, with special concern for women and children. Even though these laws do not conform exactly everywhere and in all respects to Leo's recommendations, still it is undeniable that much in them savors of the encyclical, *On the Condition of Workers*, to which great credit must be given for whatever improvement has been achieved in the workers' condition.

---

[20]Ibid. § 54.

# 3. What the Parties Directly Concerned Have Done

**29.** Finally, the wise Pontiff showed that "employers and workers themselves can accomplish much in this matter, manifestly through those institutions by the help of which the poor are opportunely assisted and the two classes of society are brought closer to each other."[21] First place among these institutions, he declares, must be assigned to associations that embrace either workers alone or workers and employers together. He goes into considerable detail in explaining and commending these associations and expounds with a truly wonderful wisdom their nature, purpose, timeliness, rights, duties, and regulations.

**30.** These teachings were issued indeed most opportunely. For at that time in many nations those at the helm of state, plainly imbued with Liberalism, were showing little favor to workers' associations of this type; nay, rather they openly opposed them, and while going out of their way to recognize similar organizations of other classes and show favor to them, they were with criminal injustice denying the natural right to form associations to those who needed it most to defend themselves from ill treatment at the hands of the powerful. There were even some Catholics who looked askance at the efforts of workers to form associations of this type as if they smacked of a socialistic or revolutionary spirit.

## Workers' Associations

**31.** The rules, therefore, which Leo XIII issued in virtue of his authority, deserve the greatest praise in that they have been able to break down this hostility and dispel these suspicions; but they have even a higher claim to distinction in that they encouraged Christian workers to found mutual associations according to their various occupations, taught them how to do so, and resolutely confirmed in the path of duty a goodly number of those to whom socialist organizations strongly attracted by claiming to be the sole defenders and champions of the lowly and oppressed.

**32.** With respect to the founding of these societies, the encyclical *On the Condition of Workers* most fittingly declared that

> workers' associations ought to be so constituted and so governed as to furnish the most suitable and most convenient means to attain the object proposed, which consists in this, that the individual mem-

---

[21] Ibid. § 68.

bers of the association secure, so far as possible, an increase in the goods of body, of soul, and of prosperity.

Yet it is clear that "moral and religious perfection ought to be regarded as their principal goal, and that their social organization as such ought above all to be directed completely by this goal.[22] For "when the regulations of associations are founded upon religion, the way is easy toward establishing the mutual relations of the members, so that peaceful living together and prosperity will result."[23]

33. To the founding of these associations the clergy and many of the laity devoted themselves everywhere with truly praiseworthy zeal, eager to bring Leo's program to full realization. Thus associations of this kind have molded truly Christian workers who, in combining harmoniously the diligent practice of their occupation with the salutary precepts of religion, protect effectively and resolutely their own temporal interests and rights, keeping a due respect for justice and a genuine desire to work together with other classes of society for the Christian renewal of all social life.

34. These counsels and instructions of Leo XIII were put into effect differently in different places according to varied local conditions. In some places one and the same association undertook to attain all the ends laid down by the Pontiff; in others, because circumstances suggested or required it, a division of work developed and separate associations were formed. Of these, some devoted themselves to the defense of the rights and legitimate interests of their members in the labor market; others took over the work of providing mutual economic aid; finally, still others gave all their attention to the fulfillment of religious and moral duties and other obligations of like nature.

35. This second method has especially been adopted where either the laws of a country, of certain special economic institutions, or that deplorable dissension of minds and hearts so widespread in contemporary society and an urgent necessity of combating with united purpose and strength the massed ranks of revolutionarists, have prevented Catholics from founding purely Catholic labor unions. Under these conditions, Catholics seem almost forced to join secular labor unions. These unions, however, should always profess justice and equity and give Catholic members full freedom to care for their own conscience and obey the laws of the Church. It is clearly the office of bishops, when they know that these associations are on account of circumstances necessary and are not dangerous to religion, to approve of Catholic workers joining them, keeping before their eyes, however, the principles and precautions laid down by our predecessor, Pius X

---

[22]Ibid. § 77.
[23]Ibid. § 78.

of holy memory.[24] Among these precautions the first and chief is this: Side by side with these unions there should always be associations zealously engaged in imbuing and forming their members in the teaching of religion and morality so that they in turn may be able to permeate the unions with that good spirit which should direct them in all their activity. As a result, the religious associations will bear good fruit even beyond the circle of their own membership.

**36.** To the encyclical of Leo, therefore, must be given this credit, that these associations of workers have so flourished everywhere that while, alas, still surpassed in numbers by socialist and communist organizations, they already embrace a vast multitude of workers and are able, within the confines of each nation as well as in wider assemblies, to maintain vigorously the rights and legitimate demands of Catholic workers and insist also on the salutary Christian principles of society.

## Associations in Other Classes

**37.** Leo's learned treatment and vigorous defense of the natural right to form associations began, furthermore, to find ready application to other associations also and not alone to those of the workers. Hence no small part of the credit must, it seems, be given to this same encyclical of Leo for the fact that among farmers and others of the middle class most useful associations of this kind are seen flourishing to a notable degree and increasing day by day, as well as other institutions of a similar nature in which spiritual development and economic benefit are happily combined.

## Associations of Employers

**38.** But if this cannot be said of organizations which our same predecessor intensely desired established among employers and managers of industry—and we certainly regret that they are so few—the condition is not wholly due to the will of men but to far graver difficulties that hinder associations of this kind which we know well and estimate at their full value. There is, however, strong hope that these obstacles also will be removed soon, and even now we greet with the deepest joy of our soul, certain by no means insignificant attempts in this direction, the rich fruits of which promise a still richer harvest in the future.[25]

---

[24]Pius X, encyclical, *Singulari Quadam*, Sept. 24, 1912.
[25]Cf. the Letter of the Sacred Congregation of the Council to the Bishop of Lille, June 5, 1929.

# Conclusion: On the Condition of Workers, the Magna Charta of the Social Order

**39.** All these benefits of Leo's encyclical, venerable brethren and beloved children, which we have outlined rather than fully described, are so numerous and of such import as to show plainly that this immortal document does not exhibit a merely fanciful, even if beautiful, ideal of human society. Rather did our predecessor draw from the Gospel and, therefore, from an everliving and life-giving fountain, teachings capable of greatly mitigating, if not immediately terminating that deadly internal struggle which is rending the family of mankind. The rich fruits which the Church of Christ and the whole human race have, by God's favor, reaped therefrom unto salvation prove that some of this good seed, so lavishly sown 40 years ago, fell on good ground. On the basis of the long period of experience, it cannot be rash to say that Leo's encyclical has proved itself the *Magna Charta* upon which all Christian activity in the social field ought to be based, as on a foundation. And those who would seem to hold in little esteem this papal encyclical and its commemoration either blaspheme what they know not, or understand nothing of what they are only superficially acquainted with, or if they do understand convict themselves formally of injustice and ingratitude.

**40.** Yet since in the course of these same years, certain doubts have arisen concerning either the correct meaning of some parts of Leo's encyclical or conclusions to be deduced therefrom, which doubts in turn have even among Catholics given rise to controversies that are not always peaceful; and since, furthermore, new needs and changed conditions of our age have made necessary a more precise application of Leo's teaching or even certain additions thereto, we most gladly seize this fitting occasion, in accord with our apostolic office through which we are debtors to all,[26] to answer, so far as in us lies, these doubts and these demands of the present day.

## II. The Authority of the Church in Social and Economic Matters

**41.** Yet before proceeding to explain these matters, that principle which Leo XIII so clearly established must be laid down at the outset here, namely, that there resides in us the right and duty to pronounce with supreme authority upon social and economic matters.[27] Certainly

---

[26]Cf. Rom 1:14.
[27]Cf. Encyclical, *On the Condition of Workers*, §§ 24-25.

the Church was not given the commission to guide men to an only fleeting and perishable happiness but to that which is eternal. Indeed "the Church holds that it is unlawful for her to mix without cause in these temporal concerns"[28]; however, she can in no wise renounce the duty God entrusted to her to interpose her authority, not of course in matters of technique for which she is neither suitably equipped nor endowed by office, but in all things that are connected with the moral law. For as to these, the deposit of truth that God committed to us and the grave duty of disseminating and interpreting the whole moral law, and of urging it in season and out of season, bring under and subject to our supreme jurisdiction not only social order but economic activities themselves.

**42.** Even though economics and moral science employs each its own principles in its own sphere, it is, nevertheless, an error to say that the economic and moral orders are so distinct from and alien to each other that the former depends in no way on the latter. Certainly the laws of economics, as they are termed, being based on the very nature of material things and on the capacities of the human body and mind, determine the limits of what productive human effort cannot, and of what it can attain in the economic field and by what means. Yet it is reason itself that clearly shows, on the basis of the individual and social nature of things and of men, the purpose which God ordained for all economic life.

**43.** But it is only the moral law which, just as it commands us to seek our supreme and last end in the whole scheme of our activity, so likewise commands us to seek directly in each kind of activity those purposes which we know that nature, or rather God the Author of nature, established for that kind of action, and in orderly relationship to subordinate such immediate purposes to our supreme and last end. If we faithfully observe this law, then it will follow that the particular purposes, both individual and social, that are sought in the economic field will fall in their proper place in the universal order of purposes, and we, in ascending through them, as it were by steps, shall attain the final end of all things, that is God, to himself and to us, the supreme and inexhaustible Good.

## 1. On Ownership or the Right of Property

**44.** But to come down to particular points, we shall begin with ownership or the right of property. Venerable brethren and beloved children, you know that our predecessor of happy memory strongly defended the right of property against the tenets of the Socialists of his time by showing that its abolition would result, not to the advan-

---

[28] Pius XI, encyclical, *Ubi Arcano*, Dec. 23, 1922.

tage of the working class, but to their extreme harm. Yet since there are some who calumniate the Supreme Pontiff, and the Church herself, as if she had taken and were still taking the part of the rich against the nonowning workers—certainly no accusation is more unjust than that—and since Catholics are at variance with one another concerning the true and exact mind of Leo, it has seemed best to vindicate this, that is, the Catholic teaching on this matter from calumnies and safeguard it from false interpretations.

## Its Individual and Social Character

**45.** First, then, let it be considered as certain and established that neither Leo nor those theologians who have taught under the guidance and authority of the Church have ever denied or questioned the twofold character of ownership, called usually individual or social according as it regards either separate persons or the common good. For they have always unanimously maintained that nature, rather the Creator himself, has given man the right of private ownership not only that individuals may be able to provide for themselves and their families but also that the goods which the Creator destined for the entire family of mankind may through this institution truly serve this purpose. All this can be achieved in no wise except through the maintenance of a certain and definite order.

**46.** Accordingly, twin rocks of shipwreck must be carefully avoided. For, as one is wrecked upon, or comes close to, what is known as *individualism* by denying or minimizing the social and public character of the right of property, so by rejecting or minimizing the private and individual character of this same right, one inevitably runs into *collectivism* or at least closely approaches its tenets. Unless this is kept in mind, one is swept from his course upon the shoals of that moral, juridical, and social modernism which we denounced in the encyclical issued at the beginning of our pontificate.[29] And, in particular, let those realize this who, in their desire for innovation, do not scruple to reproach the Church with infamous calumnies, as if she had allowed to creep into the teachings of her theologians a pagan concept of ownership which must be completely replaced by another that they with amazing ignorance call Christian.

## Obligations Inherent in Ownership

**47.** In order to place definite limits on the controversies that have arisen over ownership and its inherent duties there must be first laid down as a foundation a principle established by Leo XIII: The right

---

[29]Ibid.

of property is distinct from its use.[30] That justice called commutative commands sacred respect for the division of possessions and forbids invasion of others' rights through the exceeding of the limits of one's own property; but the duty of owners to use their property only in a right way does not come under this type of justice, but under other virtues, obligations of which "cannot be enforced by legal action."[31] Therefore, they are in error who assert that ownership and its right use are limited by the same boundaries; and it is much farther still from the truth to hold that a right to property is destroyed or lost by reason of abuse or nonuse.

**48.** Those, therefore, are doing a work that is truly salutary and worthy of all praise who, while preserving harmony among themselves and the integrity of the traditional teaching of the Church, seek to define the inner nature of these duties and their limits whereby either the right of property itself or its use, that is, the exercise of ownership, is circumscribed by the necessities of social living. On the other hand, those who seek to restrict the individual character of ownership to such a degree that in fact they destroy it are mistaken and in error.

## What the State Can Do

**49.** It follows from what we have termed the individual and at the same time social character of ownership, that men must consider in this matter not only their own advantage but also the common good. To define these duties in detail when necessity requires and the natural law has not done so, is the function of those in charge of the state. Therefore, public authority, under the guiding light always of the natural and divine law, can determine more accurately upon consideration of the true requirements of the common good, what is permitted and what is not permitted to owners in the use of their property. Moreover, Leo XIII wisely taught "that God has left the limits of private possessions to be fixed by the industry of men and institutions of peoples."[32] That history proves ownership, like other elements of social life, to be not absolutely unchanging, we once declared as follows:

> What divers forms has property had, from that primitive form among rude and savage peoples, which may be observed in some places even in our time, to the form of possession in the patriarchal age; and so further to the various forms under tyranny (we are using the word tyranny in its classical sense); and then through the feudal

---

[30] Encyclical, *On the Condition of Workers*, § 35.
[31] Ibid. § 36.
[32] Ibid. § 14.

and monarchial forms down to the various types which are to be found in more recent times.[33]

That the state is not permitted to discharge its duty arbitrarily is, however, clear. The natural right itself both of owning goods privately and of passing them on by inheritance ought always to remain intact and inviolate, since this indeed is a right that the state cannot take away: "For man is older than the state,"[34] and also, "domestic living together is prior both in thought and in fact to uniting into a polity."[35] Wherefore the wise Pontiff declared that it is grossly unjust for a state to exhaust private wealth through the weight of imposts and taxes. "For since the right of possessing goods privately has been conferred not by man's law, but by nature, public authority cannot abolish it, but can only control its exercise and bring it into conformity with the commonweal."[36] Yet when the state brings private ownership into harmony with the needs of the common good, it does not commit a hostile act against private owners but rather does them a friendly service; for it thereby effectively prevents the private possession of goods, which the Author of nature in his most wise providence ordained for the support of human life, from causing intolerable evils and thus rushing to its own destruction; it does not destroy private possessions, but safeguards them; and it does not weaken private property rights, but strengthens them.

### Obligations with Respect to Superfluous Income

**50.** Furthermore, a person's superfluous income, that is, income which he does not need to sustain life fittingly and with dignity, is not left wholly to his own free determination. Rather the Sacred Scriptures and the Fathers of the Church constantly declare in the most explicit language that the rich are bound by a very grave precept to practice almsgiving, beneficence, and munificence.
**51.** Expending larger incomes so that opportunity for gainful work may be abundant, provided, however, that this work is applied to producing really useful goods, ought to be considered, as we deduce from the principles of the Angelic Doctor,[37] an outstanding exemplification of the virtue of munificence and one particularly suited to the needs of the times.

---

[33] Allocation to the Convention of Italian Catholic Action, May 16, 1926.
[34] Encyclical, *On the Condition of Workers*, § 12.
[35] Ibid. § 20.
[36] Ibid. § 67.
[37] Cf. St. Thomas, *Summa theologica*, II-II, Q. 134.

**52.** That ownership is originally acquired both by occupancy of a thing not owned by any one and by labor, or, as is said, by specification, the tradition of all ages as well as the teaching of our predecessor Leo clearly testifies. For, whatever some idly say to the contrary, no injury is done to any person when a thing is occupied that is available to all but belongs to no one; however, only that labor which a man performs in his own name and by virtue of which a new form or increase has been given to a thing grants him title to these fruits.

## 2. Property (Capital) and Labor

**53.** Far different is the nature of work that is hired out to others and expended on the property of others. To this indeed especially applies what Leo XIII says is "incontestable," namely, that "the wealth of nations originates from no other source than from the labor of workers."[38] For is it not plain that the enormous volume of goods that makes up human wealth is produced by and issues from the hands of the workers that either toil unaided or have their efficiency marvelously increased by being equipped with tools or machines? Every one knows, too, that no nation has ever risen out of want and poverty to a better and nobler condition save by the enormous and combined toil of all the people, both those who manage work and those who carry out directions. But it is no less evident that, had not God the Creator of all things, in keeping with his goodness, first generously bestowed natural riches and resources—the wealth and forces of nature—such supreme efforts would have been idle and vain, indeed could never even have begun. For what else is work but to use or exercise the energies of mind and body on or through these very things? And in the application of natural resources to human use the law of nature, or rather God's will promulgated by it, demands that right order be observed. This order consists in this: that each thing have its proper owner. Hence it follows that unless a man is expending labor on his own property, the labor of one person and the property of another must be associated, for neither can produce anything without the other. Leo XIII certainly had this in mind when he wrote: "Neither capital can do without labor, nor labor without capital."[39] Wherefore it is wholly false to ascribe to property alone or to labor alone whatever has been obtained through the combined effort of

---

[38] Encyclical, *On the Condition of Workers*, § 51.
[39] Ibid. § 28.

both, and it is wholly unjust for either, denying the efficacy of the other, to arrogate to itself whatever has been produced.

## Unjust Claims of Capital

**54.** Property, that is, capital, has undoubtedly long been able to appropriate too much to itself. Whatever was produced, whatever returns accrued, capital claimed, for itself, hardly leaving to the worker enough to restore and renew his strength. For the doctrine was preached that all accumulation of capital falls by an absolutely insuperable economic law to the rich, and that by the same law the workers are given over and bound to perpetual want, to the scantiest of livelihoods. It is true, indeed, that things have not always and everywhere corresponded with this sort of teaching of the so-called Manchesterian Liberals; yet it cannot be denied that economic-social institutions have moved steadily in that direction. That these false ideas, these erroneous suppositions, have been vigorously assailed, and not by those alone who through them were being deprived of their innate right to obtain better conditions, will surprise no one.

## Unjust Claims of Labor

**55.** And therefore, to the harassed workers there have come intellectuals, as they are called, setting up in opposition to a fictitious law the equally fictitious moral principle that all products and profits, save only enough to repair and renew capital, belong by very right to the workers. This error, much more specious than that of certain of the Socialists who hold that whatever serves to produce goods ought to be transferred to the state, or, as they say socialized, is consequently all the more dangerous and the more apt to deceive the unwary. It is an alluring poison which many have eagerly drunk whom open Socialism had not been able to deceive.

## The Guiding Principle of Just Distribution

**56.** Unquestionably, so as not to close against themselves the road to justice and peace through these false tenets, both parties ought to have been forewarned by the wise words of our predecessor: "However the earth may be apportioned among private owners, it does not cease to serve the common interests of all."[40] This same doctrine we ourselves also taught above in declaring that the division of goods which results from private ownership was established by nature itself in order that created things may serve the needs of mankind in fixed

---

[40]Ibid. § 14.

and stable order. Lest one wander from the straight path of truth, this is something that must be continually kept in mind.

**57.** But not every distribution among human beings of property and wealth is of a character to attain either completely or to a satisfactory degree of perfection the end which God intends. Therefore, the riches that economic-social developments constantly increase ought to be so distributed among individual persons and classes that the common advantage of all, which Leo XIII had praised, will be safeguarded; in other words, that the common good of all society will be kept inviolate. By this law of social justice, one class is forbidden to exclude the other from sharing in the benefits. Hence the class of the wealthy violates this law no less, when, as if free from care on account of its wealth, it thinks it the right order of things for it to get everything and the worker nothing, than does the nonowning working class when, angered deeply at outraged justice and too ready to assert wrongly the one right it is conscious of, it demands for itself everything as if produced by its own hands, and attacks and seeks to abolish, therefore, all property and returns or incomes, of whatever kind they are or whatever the function they perform in human society, that have not been obtained by labor, and for no other reason save that they are of such a nature. And in this connection we must not pass over the unwarranted and unmerited appeal made by some to the apostle when he said: "If any man will not work neither let him eat."[41] For the apostle is passing judgment on those who are unwilling to work, although they can and ought to, and he admonishes us that we ought diligently to use our time and energies of body and mind and not be a burden to others when we can provide for ourselves. But the apostle in no wise teaches that labor is the sole title to a living or an income.[42]

**58.** To each, therefore, must be given his own share of goods, and the distribution of created goods, which, as every discerning person knows, is laboring today under the gravest evils due to the huge disparity between the few exceedingly rich and the unnumbered propertyless, must be effectively called back to and brought into conformity with the norms of the common good, that is, social justice.

## 3. Redemption of the Nonowning Workers

**59.** The redemption of the nonowning workers—this is the goal that our predecessor declared must necessarily be sought. And the point is the more emphatically to be asserted and more insistently repeated because the commands of the Pontiff, salutary as they are, have not

---

[41]2 Thes 3:10.
[42]Cf. 2 Thes 3:8-10.

infrequently been consigned to oblivion either because they were deliberately suppressed by silence or thought impracticable although they both can and ought to be put into effect. And these commands have not lost their force and wisdom for our time because that *pauperism* which Leo XIII beheld in all its horror is less widespread. Certainly the condition of the workers has been improved and made more equitable especially in the more civilized and wealthy countries where the workers can no longer be considered universally overwhelmed with misery and lacking the necessities of life. But since manufacturing and industry have so rapidly pervaded and occupied countless regions, not only in the countries called new, but also in the realms of the Far East that have been civilized from antiquity, the number of the nonowning working poor has increased enormously and their groans cry to God from the earth. Added to them is the huge army of rural wage workers, pushed to the lowest level of existence and deprived of all hope of ever acquiring "some property in land,"[43] and, therefore, permanently bound to the status of nonowning worker unless suitable and effective remedies are applied.

### Nonowning Status to Be Overcome through the Nonowning Workers Obtaining Property

**60.** Yet while it is true that the status of nonowning worker is to be carefully distinguished from pauperism, nevertheless the immense multitude of the nonowning workers on the one hand and the enormous riches of certain very wealthy men on the other establish an unanswerable argument that the riches which are so abundantly produced in our age of *industrialism*, as it is called, are not rightly distributed and equitably made available to the various classes of the people.

**61.** Therefore, with all our strength and effort we must strive that at least in the future the abundant fruits of production will accrue equitably to those who are rich and will be distributed in ample sufficiency among the workers—not that these may become remiss in work, for man is born to labor as the bird to fly—but that they may increase their property by thrift, that they may bear, by wise management of this increase in property, the burdens of family life with greater ease and security, and that, emerging from that insecure lot in life in whose uncertainties nonowning workers are cast, they may be able not only to endure the vicissitudes of earthly existence but have also assurance that when their lives are ended they will provide in some measure for those they leave after them.

---

[43]Encyclical, *On the Condition of Workers*, § 66.

**62.** All these things which our predecessor has not only suggested but clearly and openly proclaimed, we emphasize with renewed insistence in our present encyclical; and unless utmost efforts are made without delay to put them into effect, let no one persuade himself that public order, peace, and the tranquillity of human society can be effectively defended against agitators of revolution.

## 4. Just Wages and Salaries

**63.** As we have already indicated, following in the footsteps of our predecessor, it will be impossible to put these principles into practice unless the nonowning workers through industry and thrift advance to the state of possessing some little property. But except from pay for work, from what source can a man who has nothing else but work from which to obtain food and the necessaries of life set anything aside for himself through practicing frugality? Let us, therefore, explaining and developing wherever necessary Leo XIII's teachings and precepts, take up this question of wages and salaries which he called one "of very great importance."[44]

### Working for Wages Not Essentially Wrong

**64.** First of all, those who declare that a contract of hiring and being hired is unjust of its own nature, and hence a partnership-contract must take its place, are certainly in error and gravely misrepresent our predecessor whose encyclical not only accepts working for wages or salaries but deals at some length with its regulation in accordance with the rules of justice.

**65.** We consider it more advisable, however, in the present condition of human society that, so far as is possible, the work-contract be somewhat modified by a partnership-contract, as is already being done in various ways and with no small advantage to workers and owners. Workers and other employees thus become sharers in ownership or management or participate in some fashion in the profits received.

**66.** The just amount of pay, however, must be calculated not on a single basis but on several, as Leo XIII already wisely declared in these words: "To establish a rule of pay in accord with justice, many factors must be taken into account."[45]

**67.** By this statement he plainly condemned the shallowness of those who think that this most difficult matter is easily solved by the application of a single rule or measure—and one quite false.

---

[44]Ibid. § 61.
[45]Ibid. § 31.

**68.** For they are greatly in error who do not hesitate to spread the principle that labor is worth and must be paid as much as its products are worth, and that consequently the one who hires out his labor has the right to demand all that is produced through his labor. How far this is from the truth is evident from what we have already explained in treating of property and labor.

## The Individual and Social Character of Work

**69.** It is obvious that, as in the case of ownership, so in the case of work, especially work hired out to others, there is a social aspect also to be considered in addition to the personal or individual aspect. For man's productive effort cannot yield its fruits unless a truly social and organic body exists, unless a social and juridical order watches over the exercise of work, unless the various occupations, being interdependent, cooperate with and mutually complete one another, and, what is still more important, unless mind, material things, and work combine and form as it were a single whole. Therefore, where the social and individual nature of work is neglected, it will be impossible to evaluate work justly and pay it according to justice.

## Three Points to Be Considered

**70.** Conclusions of the greatest importance follow from this two-fold character which nature has impressed on human work, and it is in accordance with these that wages ought to be regulated and established.

### a) Support of the Worker and His Family
**71.** In the first place, the worker must be paid a wage sufficient to support him and his family.[46] That the rest of the family should also contribute to the common support, according to the capacity of each, is certainly right, as can be observed especially in the families of farmers, but also in the families of many craftsmen and small shopkeepers. But to abuse the years of childhood and the limited strength of women is grossly wrong. Mothers, concentrating on household duties, should work primarily in the home or in its immediate vicinity. It is an intolerable abuse, and to be abolished at all cost, for mothers on account of the father's low wage to be forced to engage in gainful occupations outside the home to the neglect of their proper cares and duties, especially the training of children. Every effort must therefore be made that fathers of families receive a wage large enough to meet ordinary family needs adequately. But if this cannot always be done

---

[46]Cf. Encyclical, *Casti Connubii*, Dec. 31, 1930.

under existing circumstances, social justice demands that changes be introduced as soon as possible whereby such a wage will be assured to every adult workingman. It will not be out of place here to render merited praise to all, who with a wise and useful purpose, have tried and tested various ways of adjusting the pay for work to family burdens in such a way that, as these increase, the former may be raised and indeed, if the contingency arises, there may be enough to meet extraordinary needs.

*b) Condition of the Business*
**72.** In determining the amount of the wage, the condition of a business and of the one carrying it on must also be taken into account; for it would be unjust to demand excessive wages which a business cannot stand without its ruin and consequent calamity to the workers. If, however, a business makes too little money, because of lack of energy or lack of initiative or because of indifference to technical and economic progress, that must not be regarded a just reason for reducing the compensation of the workers. But if the business in question is not making enough money to pay the workers an equitable wage because it is being crushed by unjust burdens or forced to sell its product at less than a just price, those who are thus the cause of the injury are guilty of grave wrong, for they deprive workers of their just wage and force them under the pinch of necessity to accept a wage less than fair.
**73.** Let, then, both workers and employers strive with united strength and counsel to overcome the difficulties and obstacles and let a wise provision on the part of public authority aid them in so salutary a work. If, however, matters come to an extreme crisis, it must be finally considered whether the business can continue or the workers are to be cared for in some other way. In such a situation, certainly most serious, a feeling of close relationship and a Christian concord of minds ought to prevail and function effectively among employers and workers.

*c) Requirements of the Common Good*
**74.** Lastly, the amount of the pay must be adjusted to the public economic good. We have shown above how much it helps the common good for workers and other employees, by setting aside some part of their income which remains after necessary expenditures, to attain gradually to the possession of a moderate amount of wealth. But another point, scarcely less important, and especially vital in our times, must not be overlooked: namely, that the opportunity to work be provided to those who are able and willing to work. This opportunity depends largely on the wage and salary rate, which can help as long as it is kept within proper limits, but which on the other hand can be an obstacle if it exceeds these limits. For everyone knows that

an excessive lowering of wages, or their increase beyond due measure, causes unemployment. This evil, indeed, especially as we see it prolonged and injuring so many during the years of our pontificate, has plunged workers into misery and temptations, ruined the prosperity of nations, and put in jeopardy the public order, peace, and tranquillity of the whole world. Hence it is contrary to social justice when, for the sake of personal gain and without regard for the common good, wages and salaries are excessively lowered or raised; and this same social justice demands that wages and salaries be so managed, through agreement of plans and wills, in so far as can be done, as to offer to the greatest possible number the opportunity of getting work and obtaining suitable means of livelihood.

**75.** A right proportion among wages and salaries also contributes directly to the same result; and with this is closely connected a right proportion in the prices at which the goods are sold that are produced by the various occupations, such as agriculture, manufacturing, and others. If all these relations are properly maintained, the various occupations will combine and coalesce into, as it were, a single body and like members of the body mutually aid and complete one another. For then only will the social economy be rightly established and attain its purposes when all and each are supplied with all the goods that the wealth and resources of nature, technical achievement, and the social organization of economic life can furnish. And these goods ought indeed to be enough both to meet the demands of necessity and decent comfort and to advance people to that happier and fuller condition of life which, when it is wisely cared for, is not only no hindrance to virtue but helps it greatly.[47]

## 5. Social Order to Be Restored

**76.** What we have thus far stated regarding an equitable distribution of property and regarding just wages concerns individual persons and only indirectly touches social order, to the restoration of which according to the principles of sound philosophy and to its perfection according to the sublime precepts of the law of the Gospel, our predecessor, Leo XIII, devoted all his thoughts and care.

**77.** Still, in order that what he so happily initiated may be solidly established, that what remains to be done may be accomplished, and that even more copious and richer benefits may accrue to the family of mankind, two things are especially necessary: reform of institutions and correction of morals.

---

[47]Cf. St. Thomas, *De regimine principum* I, 15; encyclical, *On the Condition of Workers*, §§ 49-51.

**78.** When we speak of the reform of institutions, the state comes chiefly to mind, not as if universal well-being were to be expected from its activity, but because things have come to such a pass through the evil of what we have termed *individualism*, that, following upon the overthrow and near extinction of that rich social life which was once highly developed through associations of various kinds, there remain virtually only individuals and the state. This is to the great harm of the state itself; for, with a structure of social governance lost, and with the taking over of all the burdens which the wrecked associations once bore, the state has been overwhelmed and crushed by almost infinite tasks and duties.

**79.** As history abundantly proves, it is true that on account of changed conditions many things which were done by small associations in former times cannot be done now save by large associations. Still, that most weighty principle, which cannot be set aside or changed, remains fixed and unshaken in social philosophy: Just as it is gravely wrong to take from individuals what they can accomplish by their own initiative and industry and give it to the community, so also it is an injustice and at the same time a grave evil and disturbance of right order to assign to a greater and higher association what lesser and subordinate organizations can do. For every social activity ought of its very nature to furnish help to the members of the body social, and never destroy and absorb them.

**80.** The supreme authority of the state ought, therefore, to let subordinate groups handle matters and concerns of lesser importance, which would otherwise dissipate its efforts greatly. Thereby the state will more freely, powerfully, and effectively do all those things that belong to it alone because it alone can do them: directing, watching, urging, restraining, as occasion requires and necessity demands. Therefore, those in power should be sure that the more perfectly a graduated order is kept among the various associations, in observance of the principle of *subsidiary function*, the stronger social authority and effectiveness will be and the happier and more prosperous the condition of the state.

## Mutual Cooperation of Industries and Professions

**81.** First and foremost, the state and every good citizen ought to look to and strive toward this end: that the conflict between the hostile classes be abolished and harmonious cooperation of the industries and professions be encouraged and promoted.

**82.** The social policy of the state, therefore, must devote itself to the reestablishment of the industries and professions. In actual fact, human society now, for the reason that it is founded on classes with divergent aims and hence opposed to one another and therefore inclined to enmity and strife, continues to be in a violent condition and is unstable and uncertain.

83. Labor, as our predecessor explained well in his encyclical,[48] is not a mere commodity. On the contrary, the worker's human dignity in it must be recognized. It therefore cannot be bought and sold like a commodity. Nevertheless, as the situation now stands, hiring and offering for hire in the so-called labor market separate men into two divisions, as into battle lines, and the contest between these divisions turns the labor market itself almost into a battlefield where, face to face, the opposing lines struggle bitterly. Everyone understands that this grave evil which is plunging all human society to destruction must be remedied as soon as possible. But complete cure will not come until this opposition has been abolished and well-ordered members of the social body—industries and professions—are constituted in which men may have their place, not according to the position each has in the labor market but according to the respective social functions which each performs. For under nature's guidance it comes to pass that just as those who are joined together by nearness of habitation establish towns, so those who follow the same industry or profession—whether in the economic or other field—form guilds or associations, so that many are wont to consider these self-governing organizations, if not essential, at least natural to civil society.

84. Because order, as St. Thomas well explains,[49] is unity arising from the harmonious arrangement of many objects, a true, genuine social order demands that the various members of a society be united together by some strong bond. This unifying force is present not only in the producing of goods or the rendering of services—in which the employers and employees of an identical industry or profession collaborate jointly—but also in that common good, to achieve which all industries and professions together ought, each to the best of its ability, to cooperate amicably. And this unity will be the stronger and more effective, the more faithfully individuals and the industries and professions themselves strive to do their work and excel in it.

85. It is easily deduced from what has been said that the interests common to the whole industry or profession should hold first place in these guilds. The most important among these interests is to promote the cooperation in the highest degree of each industry and profession for the sake of the common good of the country. Concerning matters, however, in which particular points, involving advantage or detriment to employers or workers, may require special care and protection, the two parties, when these cases arise, can

---

[48]Cf. Encyclical, *On the Condition of Workers*, § 31.
[49]St. Thomas, *Contra Gentiles*, III, 71; cf. *Summa theologica*, I, Q. 65, Art. 2.

deliberate separately or as the situation requires reach a decision separately.

**86.** The teaching of Leo XIII on the form of political government, namely, that men are free to choose whatever form they please, provided that proper regard is had for the requirements of justice and of the common good, is equally applicable in due proportion, it is hardly necessary to say, to the guilds of the various industries and professions.[50]

**87.** Moreover, just as inhabitants of a town are wont to found associations with the widest diversity of purposes, which each is quite free to join or not, so those engaged in the same industry or profession will combine with one another into associations equally free for purposes connected in some manner with the pursuit of the calling itself. Since these free associations are clearly and lucidly explained by our predecessor of illustrious memory, we consider it enough to emphasize this one point: People are quite free not only to found such associations, which are a matter of private order and private right, but also in respect to them "freely to adopt the organization and the rules which they judge most appropriate to achieve their purpose."[51] The same freedom must be asserted for founding associations that go beyond the boundaries of individual callings. And may these free organizations, now flourishing and rejoicing in their salutary fruits, set before themselves the task of preparing the way, in conformity with the mind of Christian social teaching, for those larger and more important guilds, industries and professions, which we mentioned before, and make every possible effort to bring them to realization.

### The Directing Principle of Economic Life to Be Restored

**88.** Attention must be given also to another matter that is closely connected with the foregoing. Just as the unity of human society cannot be founded on an opposition of classes, so also the right ordering of economic life cannot be left to a free competition of forces. For from this source, as from a poisoned spring, have originated and spread all the errors of individualist economic teaching. Destroying through forgetfulness or ignorance the social and moral character of economic life, it held that economic life must be considered and treated as altogether free from and independent of public authority, because in the market, i.e., in the free struggle of competitors, it would have a principle of self-direction which governs it much more perfectly than would the intervention of any created intellect. But free com-

---

[50]Encyclical, *Immortale Dei*, Nov. 1, 1885.
[51]Cf. encyclical, *On the Condition of Workers*, § 76.

petition, while justified and certainly useful provided it is kept within certain limits, clearly cannot direct economic life—a truth which the outcome of the application in practice of the tenets of this evil individualistic spirit has more than sufficiently demonstrated. Therefore, it is most necessary that economic life be again subjected to and governed by a true and effective directing principle. This function is one that the economic dictatorship which has recently displaced free competition can still less perform, since it is a headstrong power and a violent energy that, to benefit people, needs to be strongly curbed and wisely ruled. But it cannot curb and rule itself. Loftier and nobler principles—social justice and social charity—must, therefore, be sought whereby this dictatorship may be governed firmly and fully. Hence, the institutions themselves of peoples and, particularly those of all social life, ought to be penetrated with this justice, and it is most necessary that it be truly effective, that is, establish a juridical and social order which will, as it were, give form and shape to all economic life. Social charity, moreover, ought to be as the soul of this order, an order which public authority ought to be ever ready effectively to protect and defend. It will be able to do this the more easily as it rids itself of those burdens which, as we have stated above, are not properly its own.

**89.** Furthermore, since the various nations largely depend on one another in economic matters and need one another's help, they should strive with a united purpose and effort to promote by wisely conceived pacts and institutions a prosperous and happy international cooperation in economic life.

**90.** If the members of the body social are, as was said, reconstituted, and if the directing principle of economic-social life is restored, it will be possible to say in a certain sense even of this body what the apostle says of the mystical body of Christ: "The whole body (being closely joined and knit together through every joint of the system according to the functioning in due measure of each single part) derives its increase to the building up of itself in love."[52]

**91.** Recently, as all know, there has been inaugurated a special system of syndicates and corporations of the various callings which in view of the theme of this encyclical it would seem necessary to describe here briefly and comment upon appropriately.

**92.** The civil authority itself constitutes the syndicate as a juridical personality in such a manner as to confer on it simultaneously a certain monopoly-privilege, since only such a syndicate, when thus approved, can maintain the rights (according to the type of syndicate) of workers or employers, and since it alone can arrange for the placement of labor and conclude so-termed labor agreements. Anyone is

---

[52]Eph 4:16.

74

free to join a syndicate or not, and only within these limits can this kind of syndicate be called free; for syndical dues and special assessments are exacted of absolutely all members of every specified calling or profession, whether they are workers or employers; likewise all are bound by the labor agreements made by the legally recognized syndicate. Nevertheless, it has been officially stated that this legally recognized syndicate does not prevent the existence, without legal status however, of other associations made up of persons following the same calling.

93. The associations, or corporations, are composed of delegates from the two syndicates (that is, of workers and employers) respectively of the same industry or profession and, as true and proper organs and institutions of the state, they direct the syndicates and coordinate their activities in matters of common interest toward one and the same end.

94. Strikes and lockouts are forbidden; if the parties cannot settle their dispute, public authority intervenes.

95. Anyone who gives even slight attention to the matter will easily see what are the obvious advantages in the system we have thus summarily described: The various classes work together peacefully, socialist organizations and their activities are repressed, and a special magistracy exercises a governing authority. Yet lest we neglect anything in a matter of such great importance and that all points treated may be properly connected with the more general principles which we mentioned above and with those which we intend shortly to add, we are compelled to say that to our certain knowledge there are not wanting some who fear that the state, instead of confining itself as it ought to the furnishing of necessary and adequate assistance, is substituting itself for free activity; that the new syndical and corporative order savors too much of an involved and political system of administration; and that (in spite of those more general advantages mentioned above, which are of course fully admitted) it rather serves particular political ends than leads to the reconstruction and promotion of a better social order.

96. To achieve this latter lofty aim, and in particular to promote the common good truly and permanently, we hold it is first and above everything wholly necessary that God bless it and, secondly, that all men of good will work with united effort toward that end. We are further convinced, as a necessary consequence, that this end will be attained the more certainly the larger the number of those ready to contribute toward it their technical, occupational, and social knowledge and experience; and also, what is more important, the greater the contribution made thereto of Catholic principles and their application, not indeed by Catholic Action (which excludes strictly syndical or political activities from its scope) but by those sons of ours whom Catholic Action imbues with Catholic principles and trains for car-

rying on an apostolate under the leadership and teaching guidance of the Church—of that Church which in this field also that we have described, as in every other field where moral questions are involved and discussed, can never forget or neglect through indifference its divinely imposed mandate to be vigilant and to teach.

**97.** What we have taught about the reconstruction and perfection of social order can surely in no wise be brought to realization without reform of morality, the very record of history clearly shows. For there was a social order once which, although indeed not perfect or in all respects ideal, nevertheless, met in a certain measure the requirements of right reason, considering the conditions and needs of the time. If that order has long since perished, that surely did not happen because the order could not have accommodated itself to changed conditions and needs by development and by a certain expansion, but rather because men, hardened by too much love of self, refused to open the order to the increasing masses as they should have done, or because, deceived by allurements of a false freedom and other errors, they became impatient of every authority and sought to reject every form of control.

**98.** There remains to us, after again calling to judgment the economic system now in force and its most bitter accuser, Socialism, and passing explicit and just sentence upon them, to search out more thoroughly the root of these many evils and to point out that the first and most necessary remedy is a reform of morals.

---

## III. The Great Changes since Leo's Time

**99.** important indeed have the changes been which both the economic system and Socialism have undergone since Leo XIII's time.

**100.** That, in the first place, the whole aspect of economic life is vastly altered, is plain to all. You know, venerable brethren and beloved children, that the encyclical of our predecessor of happy memory had in view chiefly that economic system, wherein, generally, some provide capital while others provide labor for a joint economic activity. And in a happy phrase he described it thus: "Neither capital can do without labor, nor labor without capital."[53]

### 1. The Changed Aspect of Economic Life

**101.** With all his energy Leo XIII sought to adjust this economic system according to the norms of right order; hence, it is evident that

---

[53]Encyclical, *On the Condition of Workers*, § 28.

this system is not to be condemned in itself. And surely it is not of its own nature vicious. But it does violate right order when capital hires workers, that is, the nonowning working class, with a view to and under such terms that it directs business and even the whole economic system according to its own will and advantage, scorning the human dignity of the workers, the social character of economic activity and social justice itself, and the common good.

102. Even today this is not, it is true, the only economic system in force everywhere; for there is another system also, which still embraces a huge mass of humanity, significant in numbers and importance, as for example, agriculture, wherein the greater portion of mankind honorably and honestly procures its livelihood. This group, too, is being crushed with hardships and with difficulties, to which our predecessor devotes attention in several places in his encyclical and which we ourselves have touched upon more than once in our present letter.

103. But, with the diffusion of modern industry throughout the whole world, the capitalist economic regime has spread everywhere to such a degree, particularly since the publication of Leo XIII's encyclical, that it has invaded and pervaded the economic and social life of even those outside its orbit and is unquestionably impressing on it its advantages, disadvantages and vices, and, in a sense, is giving it its own shape and form.

104. Accordingly, when directing our special attention to the changes which the capitalist economic system has undergone since Leo's time, we have in mind the good not only of those who dwell in regions given over to capital and industry, but of all mankind.

**Dictatorship Has Succeeded Free Competition**

105. In the first place, it is obvious that not only is wealth concentrated in our times but an immense power and despotic economic dictatorship is consolidated in the hands of a few, who often are not owners but only the trustees and managing directors of invested funds which they administer according to their own arbitrary will and pleasure.

106. This dictatorship is being most forcibly exercised by those who, since they hold the money and completely control it, control credit also and rule the lending of money. Hence they regulate the flow, so to speak, of the lifeblood whereby the entire economic system lives, and have so firmly in their grasp the soul, as it were, of economic life that no one can breathe against their will.

107. This concentration of power and might, the characteristic mark, as it were, of contemporary economic life, is the fruit that the unlimited freedom of struggle among competitors has of its own nature produced, and which lets only the strongest survive; and this is often

the same as saying, those who fight the most violently, those who give least heed to their conscience.

**108.** This accumulation of might and of power generates in turn three kinds of conflict. First, there is the struggle for economic supremacy itself; then there is the bitter fight to gain supremacy over the state in order to use in economic struggles its resources and authority; finally there is conflict between states themselves, not only because countries employ their power and shape their policies to promote every economic advantage of their citizens, but also because they seek to decide political controversies that arise among nations through the use of their economic supremacy and strength.

## The Tragic Consequences

**109.** The ultimate consequences of the individualist spirit in economic life are those which you yourselves, venerable brethren and beloved children, see and deplore: Free competition has destroyed itself; economic dictatorship has supplanted the free market; unbridled ambition for power has likewise succeeded greed for gain; all economic life has become tragically hard, inexorable, and cruel. To these are to be added the grave evils that have resulted from an intermingling and shameful confusion of the functions and duties of public authority with those of the economic sphere—such as, one of the worst, the virtual degradation of the majesty of the state, which although it ought to sit on high like a queen and supreme arbitress, free from all partiality and intent upon the one common good and justice, is become a slave, surrendered and delivered to the passions and greed of men. And as to international relations, two different streams have issued from the one fountainhead: On the one hand, economic nationalism or even economic imperialism; on the other, a no less deadly and accursed internationalism of finance or international imperialism whose country is where profit is.

## Remedies

**110.** In the second part of this encyclical where we have presented our teaching, we have described the remedies for these great evils so explicitly that we consider it sufficient at this point to recall them briefly. Since the present system of economy is founded chiefly upon ownership and labor, the principles of right reason, that is, of Christian social philosophy, must be kept in mind regarding ownership and labor and their association together, and must be put into actual practice. First, so as to avoid the reefs of individualism and collectivism, the two-fold character, that is individual and social, both of capital or ownership and of work or labor must be given due and rightful weight. Relations of one to the other must be made to conform to the laws of strictest justice—commutative justice, as it is called—with the support, however, of Christian charity. Free competition, kept within definite and due limits, and still more economic dictatorship, must be effectively brought under public authority in these matters which pertain to the latter's function. The public institutions themselves, of peoples, moreover, ought to make all human society conform to the needs of the common good; that is, to the norm of social justice. If this is done, that most important division of social life, namely, economic activity, cannot fail likewise to return to right and sound order.

## 2. The Changes of Socialism

**111.** Socialism, against which our predecessor, Leo XIII, had especially to inveigh, has since his time changed no less profoundly than the form of economic life. For Socialism, which could then be termed almost a single system and which maintained definite teachings reduced into one body of doctrine, has since then split chiefly into two sections, often opposing each other and even bitterly hostile, without either one however abandoning a position fundamentally contrary to Christian truth that was characteristic of Socialism.

### a) The More Violent Section, or Communism

**112.** One section of Socialism has undergone almost the same change that the capitalistic economic system, as we have explained above, has undergone. It has sunk into Communism. Communism teaches and seeks two objectives: Unrelenting class warfare and absolute extermination of private ownership. Not secretly or by hidden methods does it do this, but publicly, openly and by employing every and all means, even the most violent. To achieve these objectives there is nothing which it does not dare, nothing for which it has respect or reverence; and when it has come to power, it is incredible and portent-like in its cruelty and inhumanity. The horrible slaughter and destruction through which it has laid waste vast regions of eastern Europe and Asia are the evidence; how much an enemy and how openly hostile it is to Holy Church and to God himself is, alas, too well proved by facts and fully known to all. Although we, therefore, deem it superfluous to warn upright and faithful children of the Church regarding the impious and iniquitous character of Communism, yet we cannot without deep sorrow contemplate the heedlessness of those who apparently make light of these impending dangers, and with sluggish inertia allow the widespread propagation of doctrine which seeks by violence and slaughter to destroy society altogether. All the more gravely to be condemned is the folly of those who neglect to remove or change the conditions that inflame the minds of peoples, and pave the way for the overthrow and destruction of society.

## b) The More Moderate Section Which Has Retained the Name Socialism

**113.** The other section, which has kept the name Socialism, is surely more moderate. It not only professes the rejection of violence but modifies and tempers to some degree, if it does not reject entirely, the class struggle and the abolition of private ownership. One might say that, terrified by its own principles and by the conclusions drawn therefrom by Communism, Socialism inclines toward and in a certain measure approaches the truths which Christian tradition has always held sacred; for it cannot be denied that its demands at times come very near those that Christian reformers of society justly insist upon.

### It Departs Somewhat from the Class Struggle and from the Abolition of Private Ownership

**114.** For if the class struggle abstains from enmities and mutual hatred, it gradually changes into an honest discussion of differences founded on a desire for justice, and if this is not that blessed social peace which we all seek, it can and ought to be the point of departure from which to move forward to the mutual cooperation of the industries and professions. So also the war declared on private ownership, more and more abated, is being so restricted that now, finally, not the possession itself of the means of production is attacked but rather a kind of sovereignty over society which ownership has, contrary to all right, seized and usurped. For such sovereignty belongs in reality not to owners but to the public authority. If the foregoing happens, it can come even to the point that imperceptibly these ideas of the more moderate Socialism will no longer differ from the desires and demands of those who are striving to remold human society on the basis of Christian principles. For certain kinds of property, it is rightly contended, ought to be reserved to the state since they carry with them a dominating power so great that it cannot without danger to the general welfare be entrusted to private individuals.

**115.** Such just demands and desires have nothing in them now which is inconsistent with Christian truth, and much less are they special to Socialism. Those who work solely toward such ends have, therefore, no reason to become socialists.

### Can a Middle Course Be Followed?

**116.** Yet let no one think that all the socialist groups or factions that are not communist have, without exception, recovered their senses to this extent either in fact or in name. For the most part they do not reject the class struggle or the abolition of ownership, but only in some degree modify them. Now if these false principles are modified and to some extent erased from the program, the question arises, or rather is raised without warrant by some, whether the principles of Christian truth cannot perhaps be also modified to some degree and be tempered so as to meet Socialism halfway and, as it were, by a middle course, come to agreement with it. There are some allured by the foolish hope that socialists in this way will be drawn to us. A vain hope! Those who want to be apostles among socialists ought to profess Christian truth whole and entire, openly and sincerely, and not connive at error in any way. If they truly wish to be heralds of the Gospel, let them above all strive to show to socialists that socialist claims, so far as they are just, are far more strongly supported by the principles of Christian faith and much more effectively promoted through the power of Christian charity.

117. But what if Socialism has really been so tempered and modified as to the class struggle and private ownership that there is in it no longer anything to be censured on these points? Has it thereby renounced its contradictory nature to the Christian religion? This is the question that holds many minds in suspense. And numerous are the Catholics who, although they clearly understand that Christian principles can never be abandoned or diminished seem to turn their eyes to the Holy See and earnestly beseech us to decide whether this form of Socialism has so far recovered from false doctrines that it can be accepted without the sacrifice of any Christian principle and in a certain sense be baptized. That we, in keeping with our fatherly solicitude, may answer their petitions, we make this pronouncement: Whether considered as a doctrine, or an historical fact, or a movement, Socialism, if it remains truly Socialism, even after it has yielded to truth and justice on the points which we have mentioned, cannot be reconciled with the teachings of the Catholic Church because its concept of society itself is utterly foreign to Christian truth.

## Its Concept of Society and Man's Social Character Is Utterly Foreign to Christian Truth

118. For, according to Christian teaching, man, endowed with a social nature, is placed on this earth so that by leading a life in society and under an authority ordained of God[54] he may fully cultivate and develop all his faculties unto the praise and glory of his Creator; and that by faithfully fulfilling the duties of his craft or other calling he may obtain for himself temporal and at the same time eternal happiness. Socialism, on the other hand, wholly ignoring and indifferent to this sublime end of both man and society, affirms that human association has been instituted for the sake of material advantage alone.

---

[54]Cf. Rom 13:1.

**119.** Because of the fact that goods are produced more efficiently by a suitable division of labor than by the scattered efforts of individuals, socialists infer that economic activity, only the material ends of which enter into their thinking, ought of necessity to be carried on socially. Because of this necessity, they hold that men are obliged, with respect to the producing of goods, to surrender and subject themselves entirely to society. Indeed, possession of the greatest possible supply of things that serve the advantages of this life is considered of such great importance that the higher goods of man, liberty not excepted, must take a secondary place and even be sacrificed to the demands of the most efficient production of goods. This damage to human dignity, undergone in the "socialized" process of production, will be easily offset, they say, by the abundance of socially produced goods which will pour out in profusion to individuals to be used freely at their pleasure for comforts and cultural development. Society, therefore, as Socialism conceives it, can on the one hand neither exist nor be thought of without an obviously excessive use of force; on the other hand, it fosters a liberty no less false, since there is no place in it for true social authority, which rests not on temporal and material advantages but descends from God alone, the Creator and last end of all things.[55]

## Catholic and Socialist Are Contradictory Terms

**120.** If Socialism, like all errors, contains some truth (which, moreover, the Supreme Pontiffs have never denied), it is based nevertheless on a theory of human society peculiar to itself and irreconcilable with true Christianity. Religious socialism, Christian socialism, are contradictory terms; no one can be at the same time a good Catholic and a true socialist.

## Socialism Pervading Morality and Culture

**121.** All these admonitions which have been renewed and confirmed by our solemn authority must likewise be applied to a certain new kind of socialist activity, hitherto little known but now carried on among many socialist groups. It devotes itself above all to the training of the mind and character. Under the guise of affection it tries in particular to attract children of tender age and win them to itself, although it also embraces the whole population in its scope in order finally to produce true socialists who would shape human society to the tenets of Socialism.

**122.** Since in our encyclical, *The Christian Education of Youth*,[56] we have fully taught the principles that Christian education insists on and the

---

[55]Cf. Encyclical, *Diuturnum illud*, June 29, 1881.
[56]Encyclical, *Divini illius Magistri*, Dec. 31, 1929.

82

ends it pursues, the contradiction between these principles and ends and the activities and aims of this Socialism that is pervading morality and culture is so clear and evident that no demonstration is required here. But they seem to ignore or underestimate the grave dangers that it carries with it who think it of no importance courageously and zealously to resist them according to the gravity of the situation. It belongs to our pastoral office to warn these persons of the grave and imminent evil: let all remember that Liberalism is the father of this Socialism that is pervading morality and culture and that Bolshevism will be its heir.

## Catholic Deserters to the Socialist Camp

**123.** Accordingly, venerable brethren, you can well understand with what great sorrow we observe that not a few of our sons, in certain regions especially, although we cannot be convinced that they have given up the true faith and right will, have deserted the camp of the Church and gone over to the ranks of Socialism, some to glory openly in the name of socialist and to profess socialist doctrines, others through thoughtlessness or even, almost against their wills to join associations which are socialist by profession or in fact.

**124.** In the anxiety of our paternal solicitude, we give ourselves to reflection and try to discover how it could happen that they should go so far astray and we seem to hear what many of them answer and plead in excuse: The Church and those proclaiming attachment to the Church favor the rich, neglect the workers and have no concern for them; therefore, to look after themselves they had to join the ranks of Socialism.

**125.** It is certainly most lamentable, venerable brethren, that there have been, nay, that even now there are men who, although professing to be Catholics, are almost completely unmindful of that sublime law of justice and charity that binds us not only to render to everyone what is his but to succor brothers in need as Christ the Lord himself,[57] and—what is worse—out of greed for gain do not scruple to exploit the workers. Even more, there are men who abuse religion itself, and under its name try to hide their unjust exactions in order to protect themselves from the manifestly just demands of the workers. The conduct of such we shall never cease to censure gravely. For they are the reason why the Church could, even though undeservedly, have the appearance of and be charged with taking the part of the rich and with being quite unmoved by the necessities and hardships of those who have been deprived, as it were, of their natural inheritance. The whole history of the Church plainly demon-

---

[57]Cf. Jas 2.

strates that such appearances are unfounded and such charges unjust. The encyclical itself, whose anniversary we are celebrating, is clearest proof that it is the height of injustice to hurl these calumnies and reproaches at the Church and her teaching.

## They Are Invited to Return

**126.** Although pained by the injustice and downcast in fatherly sorrow, it is so far from our thought to repulse or to disown children who have been miserably deceived and have strayed so far from the truth and salvation that we cannot but invite them with all possible solicitude to return to the maternal bosom of the Church. May they lend ready ears to our voice, may they return whence they have left, to the home that is truly their Father's, and may they stand firm there where their own place is, in the ranks of those who, zealously following the admonitions which Leo promulgated and we have solemnly repeated, are striving to restore society according to the mind of the Church on the firmly established basis of social justice and social charity. And let them be convinced that nowhere, even on earth, can they find full happiness save with him who, being rich, became poor for our sakes that through his poverty we might become rich,[58] who was poor and in labors from his youth, who invited to himself all that labor and are heavily burdened that he might refresh them fully in the love of his heart,[59] and who, lastly, without any respect for persons will require more of them to whom more has been given[60] and "will render to everyone according to his conduct."[61]

## 3. A Renewal of Morals

**127.** Yet, if we look into the matter more carefully and more thoroughly, we shall clearly perceive that, preceding this ardently desired social restoration, there must be a renewal of the Christian spirit, from which so many immersed in economic life have, far and wide, unhappily fallen away, lest all our efforts be wasted and our house be builded not on a rock but on shifting sand.[62]

**128.** And so, venerable brethren and beloved sons, having surveyed the present economic system, we have found it laboring under the gravest of evils. We have also summoned Communism and Socialism again to judgment and have found all their forms, even the most modified, to wander far from the precepts of the Gospel.

---

[58]2 Cor 8:9.
[59]Mt 11:28.
[60]Cf Lk 12:48.
[61]Mt 16:27.
[62]Mt 7:24ff.

**129.** "Wherefore," to use the words of our predecessor, "if human society is to be healed, only a return to Christian life and institutions will heal it."[63] For this alone can provide effective remedy for that excessive care for passing things that is the origin of all vices; and this alone can draw away men's eyes, fascinated by and wholly fixed on the changing things of the world, and raise them toward Heaven. Who would deny that human society is in most urgent need of this cure now?

### The Chief Form of Disorder in the Contemporary Regime: Loss of Souls

**130.** Minds of all, it is true, are affected almost solely by temporal upheavals, disasters, and calamities. But if we examine things critically with Christian eyes, as we should, what are all these compared with the loss of souls? Yet it is not rash by any means to say that the whole scheme of social and economic life is now such as to put in the way of vast numbers of mankind most serious obstacles which prevent them from caring for the one thing necessary; namely, their eternal salvation.

**131.** We, made shepherd and protector by the Prince of Shepherds, who redeemed them by his blood, of a truly innumerable flock, cannot hold back our tears when contemplating this greatest of their dangers. Nay rather, fully mindful of our pastoral office and with paternal solicitude, we are continually meditating on how we can help them; and we have summoned to our aid the untiring zeal also of others who are concerned on grounds of justice or charity. For what will it profit men to become expert in more wisely using their wealth, even to gaining the whole world, if thereby they suffer the loss of their souls?[64] What will it profit to teach them sound principles of economic life if in unbridled and sordid greed they let themselves be swept away by their passion for property, so that "hearing the commandments of the Lord they do all things contrary."[65]

### Causes of This Loss

**132.** The root and font of this defection in economic and social life from the Christian law, and of the consequent apostasy of great numbers of workers from the Catholic faith, are the disordered passions of the soul, the sad result of original sin which has so destroyed the wonderful harmony of man's faculties that, easily led astray by his

---

[63]Encyclical, *On the Condition of Workers*, § 41.
[64]Cf. Mt 16:26.
[65]Cf. Jgs 2:17.

evil desires, he is strongly incited to prefer the passing goods of this world to the lasting goods of Heaven. Hence arises that unquenchable thirst for riches and temporal goods, which has at all times impelled men to break God's laws and trample upon the rights of their neighbors, but which, on account of the present system of economic life, is laying far more numerous snares for human frailty. Since the instability of economic life, and especially of its structure, exacts of those engaged in it most intense and unceasing effort, some have become so hardened to the stings of conscience as to hold that they are allowed, in any manner whatsoever, to increase their profits and use means, fair or foul, to protect their hard-won wealth against sudden changes of fortune. The easy gains that a market unrestricted by any law opens to everybody attracts large numbers to buying and selling goods, and they, their one aim being to make quick profits with the least expenditure of work, raise or lower prices by their uncontrolled business dealings so rapidly according to their own caprice and greed that they nullify the wisest forecasts of producers. The laws passed to promote corporate business, while dividing and limiting the risk of business, have given occasion to the most sordid license. For we observe that consciences are little affected by this reduced obligation of accountability; that furthermore, by hiding under the shelter of a joint name, the worst of injustices and frauds are perpetrated; and that, too, directors of business companies, forgetful of their trust, betray the rights of those whose savings they have undertaken to administer. Lastly, we must not omit to mention those crafty men who, wholly unconcerned about any honest usefulness of their work, do not scruple to stimulate the baser human desires and, when they are aroused, use them for their own profit.

**133.** Strict and watchful moral restraint enforced vigorously by governmental authority could have banished these enormous evils and even forestalled them; this restraint, however, has too often been sadly lacking. For since the seeds of a new form of economy were bursting forth just when the principles of rationalism had been implanted and rooted in many minds, there quickly developed a body of economic teaching far removed from the true moral law, and, as a result, completely free rein was given to human passions.

**134.** Thus it came to pass that many, much more than ever before, were solely concerned with increasing their wealth by any means whatsoever, and that in seeking their own selfish interests before everything else they had no conscience about committing even the gravest of crimes against others. Those first entering upon this broad way that leads to destruction[66] easily found numerous imitators of their iniquity by the example of their manifest success, by their inso-

---

[66] Cf. Mt 7:13.

lent display of wealth, by their ridiculing the conscience of others, who, as they said, were troubled by silly scruples, or lastly by crushing more conscientious competitors.

135. With the rulers of economic life abandoning the right road, it was easy for the rank and file of workers everywhere to rush headlong also into the same chasm; and all the more so, because very many managements treated their workers like mere tools, with no concern at all for their souls, without indeed even the least thought of spiritual things. Truly the mind shudders at the thought of the grave dangers to which the morals of workers (particularly young workers) and the modesty of girls and women are exposed in modern factories; when we recall how often the present economic scheme, and particularly the shameful housing conditions, create obstacles to the family bond and normal family life; when we remember how many obstacles are put in the way of the proper observance of Sundays and Holy Days; and when we reflect upon the universal weakening of that truly Christian sense through which even rude and unlettered men were wont to value higher things, and upon its substitution by the single preoccupation of getting in any way whatsoever one's daily bread. And thus bodily labor, which Divine Providence decreed to be performed, even after original sin, for the good at once of man's body and soul, is being everywhere changed into an instrument of perversion; for dead matter comes forth from the factory ennobled, while men there are corrupted and degraded.

**Remedies**

*a) Economic Life Should Be Given Form and Shape in Accordance with Christian Principles*

136. No genuine cure can be furnished for this lamentable ruin of souls, which, so long as it continues, will frustrate all efforts to regenerate society, unless men return openly and sincerely to the teaching of the Gospel, to the precepts of him who alone has the words of everlasting life,[67] words which will never pass away, even if Heaven and earth will pass away.[68] All experts in social problems are seeking eagerly a structure so fashioned in accordance with the norms of reason that it can lead economic life back to sound and right order. But this order, which we ourselves ardently long for and with all our efforts promote, will be wholly defective and incomplete unless all the activities of men harmoniously unite to imitate and attain, insofar as it lies within human strength, the marvelous unity of the divine plan. We mean that perfect order which the Church with great force

---

[67]Cf. Jn 6:69.
[68]Cf. Mt 24:35.

and power preaches and which right human reason itself demands, that all things be directed to God as the first and supreme end of all created activity, and that all created good under God be considered as mere instruments to be used only insofar as they conduce to the attainment of the supreme end. Nor is it to be thought that gainful occupations are thereby belittled or judged less consonant with human dignity; on the contrary, we are taught to recognize in them with reverence the manifest will of the Divine Creator who placed man upon the earth to work it and use it in a multitude of ways for his needs. Those who are engaged in producing goods, therefore, are not forbidden to increase their fortune in a just and lawful manner; for it is only fair that he who renders service to the community and makes it richer should also, through the increased wealth of the community, be made richer himself according to his position, provided that all these things be sought with due respect for the laws of God and without impairing the rights of others and that they be employed in accordance with faith and right reason. If these principles are observed by everyone, everywhere, and always, not only the production and acquisition of goods but also the use of wealth, which now is seen to be so often contrary to right order, will be brought back soon within the bounds of equity and just distribution. The sordid love of wealth, which is the shame and great sin of our age, will be opposed in actual fact by the gentle yet effective law of Christian moderation which commands man to seek first the Kingdom of God and his justice, with the assurance that, by virtue of God's kindness and unfailing promise, temporal goods also, insofar as he has need of them, shall be given him besides.[69]

## b) The Role of Charity

**137.** But in effecting all this, the law of charity, "which is the bond of perfection,"[70] must always take a leading role. How completely deceived, therefore, are those rash reformers who concern themselves with the enforcement of justice alone—and this, commutative justice—and in their pride reject the assistance of charity! Admittedly, no vicarious charity can substitute for justice which is due as an obligation and is wrongfully denied. Yet even supposing that everyone should finally receive all that is due him, the widest field for charity will always remain open. For justice alone can, if faithfully observed, remove the causes of social conflict but can never bring about union of minds and hearts. Indeed all the institutions for the establishment of peace and the promotion of mutual help among men, however perfect these may seem, have the principal foundation

---

[69]Cf. Mt 6:33.
[70]Col 3:14.

of their stability in the mutual bond of minds and hearts whereby the members are united with one another. If this bond is lacking, the best of regulations come to naught, as we have learned by too frequent experience. And so, then only will true cooperation be possible for a single common good when the constituent parts of society deeply feel themselves members of one great family and children of the same Heavenly Father; nay, that they are one body in Christ, "but severally members one of another,"[71] so that "if one member suffers anything, all the members suffer with it."[72] For then the rich and others in positions of power will change their former indifference toward their poorer brothers into a solicitous and active love, listen with kindliness to their just demands, and freely forgive their possible mistakes and faults. And the workers, sincerely putting aside every feeling of hatred or envy which the promoters of social conflict so cunningly exploit, will not only accept without rancor the place in human society assigned them by Divine Providence, but rather will hold it in esteem, knowing well that everyone according to his function and duty is toiling usefully and honorably for the common good and is following closely in the footsteps of him who, being in the form of God, willed to be a carpenter among men and be known as the son of a carpenter.

**An Arduous Task**

**138.** Therefore, out of this new diffusion throughout the world of the spirit of the Gospel, which is the spirit of Christian moderation and universal charity, we are confident there will come that longed for and full restoration of human society in Christ, and that "Peace of Christ in the Kingdom of Christ," to accomplish which, from the very beginning of our pontificate, we firmly determined and resolved within our heart to devote all our care and all our pastoral solicitude,[73] and toward this same highly important and most necessary end now, you also, venerable brethren who with us rule the Church of God under the mandate of the Holy Ghost,[74] are earnestly toiling with wholly praiseworthy zeal in all parts of the world, even in the regions of the holy missions to the infidels. Let well-merited acclamations of praise be bestowed upon you and at the same time upon all those, both clergy and laity, who we rejoice to see, are daily participating and valiantly helping in this same great work, our beloved sons engaged in Catholic Action, who with a singular zeal are undertaking with us the solution of the social problems insofar as by virtue of her divine

---

[71]Rom 12:5.
[72]1 Cor 12:26.
[73]Encyclical, *Ubi Arcano*, Dec. 23, 1922.
[74]Cf. Acts 20:28.

institution this is proper to and devolves upon the Church. All these we urge in the Lord, again and again, to spare no labors and let no difficulties conquer them, but rather to become day by day more courageous and more valiant.[75] Arduous indeed is the task which we propose to them, for we know well that on both sides, both among the upper and the lower classes of society, there are many obstacles and barriers to be overcome. Let them not, however, lose heart; to face bitter combats is a mark of Christians, and to endure grave labors to the end is a mark of them who, as good soldiers of Christ,[76] follow him closely.

139. Relying therefore solely on the all-powerful aid of him "who wishes all men to be saved,"[77] let us strive with all our strength to help those unhappy souls who have turned from God and, drawing them away from the temporal cares in which they are too deeply immersed, let us teach them to aspire with confidence to the things that are eternal. Sometimes this will be achieved much more easily than seems possible at first sight to expect. For if wonderful spiritual forces lie hidden, like sparks beneath ashes, within the secret recesses of even the most abandoned man—certain proof that his soul is naturally Christian—how much the more in the hearts of those many upon many who have been led into error rather through ignorance or environment.

140. Moreover, the ranks of the workers themselves are already giving happy and promising signs of a social reconstruction. To our soul's great joy, we see in these ranks also the massed companies of young workers, who are receiving the counsel of Divine Grace with willing ears and striving with marvelous zeal to gain their comrades for Christ. No less praise must be accorded to the leaders of workers' organizations who, disregarding their own personal advantage and concerned solely about the good of their fellow members, are striving prudently to harmonize the just demands of their members with the prosperity of their whole occupation and also to promote these demands, and who do not let themselves be deterred from so noble a service by any obstacle or suspicion. Also, as anyone may see, many young men, who by reason of their talent or wealth will soon occupy high places among the leaders of society, are studying social problems with deeper interest, and they arouse the joyful hope that they will dedicate themselves wholly to the restoration of society.

---

[75]Cf. Dt 31:7.
[76]Cf. 2 Tm 2:3.
[77]1 Tm 2:4.

**141.** The present state of affairs, venerable brethren, clearly indicates the way in which we ought to proceed. For we are now confronted, as more than once before in the history of the Church, with a world that in large part has almost fallen back into paganism. That these whole classes of men may be brought back to Christ whom they have denied, we must recruit and train from among them, themselves, auxiliary soldiers of the Church who know them well and their minds and wishes, and can reach their hearts with a tender brotherly love. The first and immediate apostle to the workers ought to be workers; the apostles to those who follow industry and trade ought to be from among them themselves.

**142.** It is chiefly your duty, venerable brethren, and of your clergy, to search diligently for these lay apostles both of workers and of employers, to select them with prudence, and to train and instruct them properly. A difficult task, certainly, is thus imposed on priests, and to meet it, all who are growing up as the hope of the Church, must be duly prepared by an intensive study of the social question. Especially is it necessary that those whom you intend to assign in particular to this work should demonstrate that they are men possessed of the keenest sense of justice, who will resist with true manly courage the dishonest demands or the unjust acts of anyone, who will excel in the prudence and judgment which avoids every extreme, and, above all, who will be deeply permeated by the charity of Christ, which alone has the power to subdue firmly but gently the hearts and wills of men to the laws of justice and equity. Upon this road so often tried by happy experience, there is no reason why we should hesitate to go forward with all speed.

**143.** These our beloved sons who are chosen for so great a work, we earnestly exhort in the Lord to give themselves wholly to the training of the men committed to their care, and in the discharge of this eminently priestly and apostolic duty to make proper use of the resources of Christian education by teaching youth, forming Christian organizations, and founding study groups guided by principles in harmony with the Faith. But above all, let them hold in high esteem and assiduously employ for the good of their disciples that most valuable means of both personal and social restoration which, as we taught in our encyclical, *Mens Nostra*,[78] is to be found in the Spiritual Exercises. In that letter we expressly mentioned and warmly recommended not only the Spiritual Exercises for all the laity, but also the highly beneficial workers' retreats. For in that school of the spirit, not only are the best of Christians developed but true apostles also

---

[78]Encyclical, *Mens Nostra*, Dec. 20, 1929.

are trained for every condition of life and are enkindled with the fire of the heart of Christ. From this school they will go forth as did the apostles from the upper room of Jerusalem, strong in faith, endowed with an invincible steadfastness in persecution, burning with zeal, interested solely in spreading everywhere the Kingdom of Christ.

**144.** Certainly there is the greatest need now of such valiant soldiers of Christ who will work with all their strength to keep the human family safe from the dire ruin into which it would be plunged were the teachings of the Gospel to be flouted, and that order of things permitted to prevail which tramples underfoot no less the laws of nature than those of God. The Church of Christ, built upon an unshakable rock, has nothing to fear for herself, as she knows for a certainty that the gates of hell shall never prevail against her.[79] Rather, she knows full well, through the experience of many centuries, that she is wont to come forth from the most violent storms stronger than ever and adorned with new triumphs. Yet her maternal heart cannot but be moved by the countless evils with which so many thousands would be afflicted during storms of this kind, and above all by the consequent enormous injury to spiritual life which would work eternal ruin to so many souls redeemed by the Blood of Jesus Christ.

**145.** To ward off such great evils from human society nothing, therefore, is to be left untried; to this end may all our labors turn, to this all our energies, to this our fervent and unremitting prayers to God! For with the assistance of Divine Grace the fate of the human family rests in our hands.

**146.** Venerable brethren and beloved sons, let us not permit the children of this world to appear wiser in their generation than we who by the Divine Goodness are the children of the light.[80] We find them, indeed, selecting and training with the greatest shrewdness alert and resolute devotees who spread their errors ever wider day by day through all classes of men and in every part of the world. And whenever they undertake to attack the Church of Christ more violently, we see them put aside their internal quarrels, assembling in full harmony in a single battle line with a completely united effort, and work to achieve their common purpose.

## Close Union and Cooperation Are Urged

**147.** Surely there is not one that does not know how many and how great are the works that the tireless zeal of Catholics is striving everywhere to carry out, both for social and economic welfare as well as in the fields of education and religion. But this admirable and un-

---

[79] Cf. Mt 16:18.
[80] Cf. Lk 16:8.

remitting activity not infrequently shows less effectiveness because of the dispersion of its energies in too many different directions. Therefore, let all men of good will stand united, all who under the shepherds of the Church wish to fight this good and peaceful battle of Christ; and under the leadership and teaching guidance of the Church let all strive according to the talent, powers, and position of each to contribute something to the Christian reconstruction of human society which Leo XIII inaugurated through his immortal encyclical, *On the Condition of Workers*, seeking not themselves and their own interests, but those of Jesus Christ,[81] not trying to press at all costs their own counsels, but ready to sacrifice them, however excellent, if the greater common good should seem to require it, so that in all and above all Christ may reign, Christ may command, to whom be "honor and glory and dominion forever and ever."[82]

**148.** That this may happily come to pass, to all of you, venerable brethren and beloved children, who are members of the vast Catholic family entrusted to us, but with the especial affection of our heart to workers and to all others engaged in manual occupations, committed to us more urgently by Divine Providence, and to Christian employers and managements, with paternal love we impart the Apostolic Benediction.

**149.** Given at Rome, at Saint Peter's, the fifteenth day of May, in the year 1931, the tenth year of our pontificate.

Pope Pius XI

---

[81]Cf. Phil 2:21.
[82]Rv 5:13.